Claudiu S. Firan

From Search Personalization to Semantic Enrichment

Claudiu S. Firan

From Search Personalization to Semantic Enrichment

Adapting Information Retrieval to User Needs in an Evolving Web Environment

Südwestdeutscher Verlag für Hochschulschriften

Impressum/Imprint (nur für Deutschland/only for Germany)
Bibliografische Information der Deutschen Nationalbibliothek: Die Deutsche Nationalbibliothek verzeichnet diese Publikation in der Deutschen Nationalbibliografie; detaillierte bibliografische Daten sind im Internet über http://dnb.d-nb.de abrufbar.
Alle in diesem Buch genannten Marken und Produktnamen unterliegen warenzeichen-, marken- oder patentrechtlichem Schutz bzw. sind Warenzeichen oder eingetragene Warenzeichen der jeweiligen Inhaber. Die Wiedergabe von Marken, Produktnamen, Gebrauchsnamen, Handelsnamen, Warenbezeichnungen u.s.w. in diesem Werk berechtigt auch ohne besondere Kennzeichnung nicht zu der Annahme, dass solche Namen im Sinne der Warenzeichen- und Markenschutzgesetzgebung als frei zu betrachten wären und daher von jedermann benutzt werden dürften.

Coverbild: www.ingimage.com

Verlag: Südwestdeutscher Verlag für Hochschulschriften GmbH & Co. KG
Dudweiler Landstr. 99, 66123 Saarbrücken, Deutschland
Telefon +49 681 37 20 271-1, Telefax +49 681 37 20 271-0
Email: info@svh-verlag.de

Zugl.: Leibniz Universität Hannover, Diss., 2010

Herstellung in Deutschland:
Schaltungsdienst Lange o.H.G., Berlin
Books on Demand GmbH, Norderstedt
Reha GmbH, Saarbrücken
Amazon Distribution GmbH, Leipzig
ISBN: 978-3-8381-2648-7

Imprint (only for USA, GB)
Bibliographic information published by the Deutsche Nationalbibliothek: The Deutsche Nationalbibliothek lists this publication in the Deutsche Nationalbibliografie; detailed bibliographic data are available in the Internet at http://dnb.d-nb.de.
Any brand names and product names mentioned in this book are subject to trademark, brand or patent protection and are trademarks or registered trademarks of their respective holders. The use of brand names, product names, common names, trade names, product descriptions etc. even without a particular marking in this works is in no way to be construed to mean that such names may be regarded as unrestricted in respect of trademark and brand protection legislation and could thus be used by anyone.

Cover image: www.ingimage.com

Publisher: Südwestdeutscher Verlag für Hochschulschriften GmbH & Co. KG
Dudweiler Landstr. 99, 66123 Saarbrücken, Germany
Phone +49 681 37 20 271-1, Fax +49 681 37 20 271-0
Email: info@svh-verlag.de

Printed in the U.S.A.
Printed in the U.K. by (see last page)
ISBN: 978-3-8381-2648-7

Copyright © 2011 by the author and Südwestdeutscher Verlag für Hochschulschriften GmbH & Co. KG and licensors
All rights reserved. Saarbrücken 2011

Contents

Table of Contents i

List of Figures v

1 **Introduction** 1
   1.1 IR Challenges and Proposed Solutions 2
   1.2 Thesis Structure 5

2 **Web IR: Background and Related Work** 7
   2.1 History of the WWW and IR 7
   2.2 Textual Information Retrieval 8
      2.2.1 Inverted Index Structure 9
      2.2.2 Ranking and *TFxIDF* Weighting 10
      2.2.3 Evaluation Metrics 11
   2.3 Search Personalization 13
      2.3.1 Personalized Search 13
      2.3.2 Automatic Query Expansion 14
      2.3.3 Just-in-Time Information Retrieval 16
      2.3.4 Summarization 17
   2.4 Web 2.0 and Multimedia IR 18
      2.4.1 Social Web Sites 18
      2.4.2 Multimedia IR Using Textual Annotations .. 20
   2.5 Tags as User Generated Content 21

	2.5.1	Tag Analyses	21
	2.5.2	Knowledge Discovery Through Tags	22
	2.5.3	Tagging Motivations and Types of Tags	23
2.6	Event Based IR		24
	2.6.1	Application Scenario	25
	2.6.2	Event Detection	26
2.7	Entity Retrieval		28
	2.7.1	Entity Retrieval Related Tasks	29
	2.7.2	Application Scenarios for ER	30
	2.7.3	Existing ER Approaches	32

3 Search Personalization for the Web 35

3.1	Introduction		35
3.2	Query Reformulation Patterns		37
3.3	Query Expansion Using Desktop Data		41
	3.3.1	Algorithms	42
	3.3.2	Introducing Adaptivity	51
3.4	Recommending Related Web Pages to User Tasks		55
	3.4.1	Extracting Relevant Query Keywords	56
	3.4.2	Recommending Related Web Pages	57
	3.4.3	Evaluation	58
3.5	Discussion		67

4 Automatic Semantic Enrichment 69

4.1	Introduction		69
4.2	Analysis of Tag Usage		72
	4.2.1	Data Set Descriptions	72
	4.2.2	Tags' Characteristics	74
	4.2.3	Usefulness of Tags for Search	78
4.3	Knowledge Discovery Through Tags		80
	4.3.1	Data Set Descriptions	81
	4.3.2	Deriving Music Moods and Themes	82
	4.3.3	Deriving Moods for Pictures	88
4.4	Event Detection from Tags		93
	4.4.1	Data Set Descriptions	94
	4.4.2	Event Detection Methods	96

| 4.4.3   Evaluation 100
| 4.5 Discussion 104

5 Conclusions and Outlook 107

Bibliography 111

List of Figures

2.1	SMART notation for $tfidf$ variants, as in [MRS08]	11
2.2	Tag cloud presenting Web 2.0 themes	19
3.1	Query reformulation patterns as a function of clarity.	38
3.2	Relative NDCG gain (in %) for each algorithm overall, as well as separated per query category.	55
3.3	Precision at 1..5 considering only the first *5* sentences of an *email* . .	62
3.4	Precision at 1..5 considering only the first *15* sentences of an *email* .	63
3.5	Precision at 1..5 considering the *entire* text of an *email*	63
3.6	Precision at 1..5 considering only the first *10* sentences of a text *document*	64
3.7	Precision at 1..5 considering only the first *25* sentences of a text *document*	64
3.8	Precision at 1..5 considering the *entire* text *document*	65
3.9	Precision at 1..5 considering the *entire* text of a *web page*	65
3.10	Mean average precision per input file type	66
4.1	Tag type distributions across systems	76
4.2	Distribution of query types for different resources	78
4.3	Mood Mates! Facebook application	89
4.4	Confusion matrices for A) primary and B) secondary emotions as image moods	92
4.5	$H@3$ and MRR values across our best music, image, mood and theme recommendations	94
4.6	Classification results (Acc, P, R) for the three experimental runs . . .	102

Introduction

The most dramatic change in the way we live our lives has been the communication over the Internet. Could you imagine your life without using the Web – no email, no access to breaking news, no up to the minute weather reports, no way to shop online? We have grown to be dependent on this technology. If we would try to live one day without using the Web in some fashion, we'll probably be surprised at how much we depend on it. For a variety of activities, people are no longer required to leave the commodity of their own homes; everything is there, at the click of a button.

The Web is a giant experiment, a global theory, that has amazingly enough worked pretty well. Its history illustrates the ways that technological advancement and innovation can move along unintended paths. Originally, the Web and the Internet were created to be part of a military strategy, and not meant for private use. However, as in many experiments, theories, and plans, its initial goal has been changed. The World Wide Web has enabled performing many more transactions, online comparisons, services, and thus totally changed the way we interact with the entire world, and has certainly overwhelmed us with information. In order to find and make use of this plethora of information, new services of Information Retrieval have become irreplaceable.

Information Retrieval research has started long before the development of the Web. The idea of using computers to search for relevant pieces of information was popularized in the article "As We May Think" by Vannevar Bush in 1945. The first automated information retrieval systems were introduced in the 1950s and 1960s. By 1970 several different techniques had been shown to perform well on small text corpora such as the Cranfield collection (several thousand documents). Large-scale retrieval systems, such as the Lockheed Dialog system, came into use early in the 1970s. Nevertheless, most of the Web IR research was done with the exponential growth of textual information on the Web and the emerging need to find focused topics. Data organization moved from directory based services – Yahoo! in the early 90s, Google Directory, Open Directory Project – to search based access to the Web as known today.

As a next step in Web evolution, the amount of user generated data overgrew the amount of expert (webmaster) generated data. Web 2.0 sites enabled all Web users to share their thoughts, experiences, basically any kind of information with all other users – former consumers became both consumers and producers, so called "prosumers". As a side effect, all this user generated information represents a very useful additional data about resources on the Web.

As bandwidth grows, the amount of audio-visual data becomes larger and the need arises once more, like once for textual IR, to retrieve all these multimedia resources efficiently. Web 2.0 user generated data became until today basically irreplaceable for resources other than text for which very little information is extractable directly and automatically from the resources themselves. Also, other presentation methods started to become more popular, starting from simple GUI modifications to structural modification in the architecture of the systems. With the rapidly increasing popularity of Social Media sites, a lot of user generated content has been injected in the Web, resulting in a large amount of both multimedia items (music – *Last.fm*, *MySpace*, pictures – *Flickr*, *Picasa*, videos – *YouTube*) and textual data (tags and other text-based documents). As a consequence, it has become more and more difficult using standard IR techniques to find exactly the content that matches the users' information needs. Organizing different media types together with textual content in the form of events became an emerging presentation model and tries to alleviate this problem.

Finding entities on the Web is also a new IR task which goes beyond the classic document search. While for informational search tasks document search can give satisfying results for the user, different approaches should be followed when the user is looking for specific entities. For example, when the user wants to find a list of "European female politicians" it is easy for a classical search engine to return documents about politics in Europe. It is left to the user to extract the information about the requested entities from the provided results. The goal of Entity Retrieval (entity based IR) is to develop a system that can find targeted entities and not just documents on the Web.

1.1 IR Challenges and Proposed Solutions

Personalization in Textual IR

Problem: ambiguous queries. The booming popularity of Web search engines has determined simple keyword search to become the only widely accepted user interface for seeking information over the Web. Yet keyword queries are inherently ambiguous. The query "canon book" for example covers several different areas of interest: religion, digital photography, literature, and music. Interestingly, this is one of the examples in which the first ten Google results do not contain any URL on the last topic. Clearly,

1.1 IR Challenges and Proposed Solutions

search engine output should be filtered to better align the results with the users interests. A study presented by SearchEngineWatch [Sul04] indicated that more than 80% of the users would prefer to receive personalized search results. Personalization algorithms accomplish this goal by (1) learning / defining users interests and (2) delivering search results customized accordingly: pages about digital cameras for the photographer, religious books for the clergyman, and documents on music theory for the performing artist.

Solution: search personalization. Therefore, we propose to exploit the user's manually created personal information repository to personalize Web search, i.e. to return search results which are relevant to the user profile and are of good quality. In this way we will improve *precision*, as this is the measure which is most meaningful in Web IR. Clearly finding every possible information is important to the user, but the vast data on the Web makes it easy to find millions of Web pages often offering redundant information. In the majority of cases, the Web user is thus not as much interested in *recall* anymore, i.e. finding all information sources, as he is in *precision*, i.e. finding first the most relevant and reliable sources.

Proposed approaches. We perform an analysis of how users reformulate their Web search queries to detect good strategies in targeting the query towards the real user information need. Then, we make use of the vast already existing information in the personal documents of the user to personalize Web queries. By several different summarization methods, we extract key terms and phrases from the user's desktop and make use of them to expand the given user query. In this way, by performing Query Expansion, we are able to focus the user query towards the real user goals, at the same time keeping all information on the user side to enforce privacy. Furthermore, we employ our summarization and text mining algorithms to assist the user when performing tasks such as writing documents or emails, or browsing Web pages. Based on the currently active user documents we recommend additional sources of information on the Web.

Annotations in Multimedia IR

Problem: underrepresented annotations. In contrast to Web IR, in Multimedia IR the system goes beyond retrieving text pages as results and presents the user resources like pictures, videos, songs, etc. Together with the Web 2.0 era and the higher availability of large bandwidth, users target more and more these richer kind of resources. Still, the user input is a simple textual query which has to be matched to multimedia objects. Search engines thus focus on extracting and attaching textual annotations to these types of objects. As extraction of audio and visual features directly from the resources is still emerging from the performance point of view, a significant source of textual information is provided by user generated annotations. Collaborative tagging as a flexible means for information organization and sharing has become highly popular in recent years. By assigning freely selectable words to bookmarked Web pages (*Del.icio.us*), to music (*Last.fm*) or pictures (*Flickr*) users generate a huge amount of semantically rich metadata. Yet the generated metadata differs from the way users search for multimedia objects [BFNP08]. Take the domain of music for example: 60% of the top user tags are genre related (e.g. "pop", "rock"), yet only 5% refer to themes (e.g. "party time", "Friday night", "driving"). In contrast, 30% of the user queries are theme-related; this makes the need obvious to create specific annotations to enable user intended resource retrieval.

Solution: semantic enrichment. Our methods automatically create focused metadata for the different types of audio-visual resources. We infer the needed and searched types of annotations from already existing information. In this way we are able to increase both *precision* – by generating high quality annotations – and *recall* – by creating additional annotations of underrepresented types –, as recall is more important here than for Web IR.

Proposed approaches. We analyze tagging behavior in different tagging systems and across different types of resources (text, music, pictures) in order to get more insight about the nature of tags and different types of tags employed. We also analyze Web queries for these types of resources and identified gaps between the tagging and the querying vocabulary. Based on these findings, we propose methods for Semantic Enrichment, i.e. automatically generate underrepresented types of annotations using the already existing information. Moreover, we also focus on event driven IR, where the resources are organized around the events they are part of, rather than out of context stand-alone resources. Our algorithms on event detection are able to discover the event a resource belongs to based on the context already provided by users (e.g. general user tags).

Contributions of this Thesis

Our various contributions to Web IR are summarized as follows:

- We provide new insights into Web users' query reformulation patterns;
- We develop several algorithms to perform efficient search personalization keeping all data private;
- We ease users' work by unobtrusively presenting relevant information to their current task;
- We analyze tagging and querying vocabularies for the major types of resources on the Web (Web pages, pictures, music);
- We automatically enrich necessary but underrepresented annotation types in order to enhance resources' descriptions for multimedia IR;
- We classify resources into events and event categories to enable a highly intuitive way of organizing and indexing media.

1.2 Thesis Structure

We start in Chapter 2 by presenting Web and IR evolution from the beginning until today. After the general description we also present the focused research done in the fields around which this thesis is centered. Following the historical background (Section 2.1) we give a general overview of Textual Information Retrieval in Section 2.2. We then, in Section 2.3, present an in-depth view of the research done in the area of Search Personalization. Another step in the evolution of the Web is the so-called Web 2.0 and the domain of Multimedia IR – presented in Section 2.4. Section 2.5 discusses the work done in the Web 2.0 area, more specifically about user generated tags, both analyses and applications to Multimedia IR. We also present two areas which go beyond pure document or resource oriented retrieval: Event Based IR in Section 2.6 and Entity Retrieval in Section 2.7. We give an overview of these two areas as well as relevant research.

Chapter 3 presents our work done in the area of Web Search Personalization. After the introduction in Section 3.1 we start with an analysis of Query Reformulation patterns in Web search (Section 3.2). Section 3.3 shows approaches for enabling Search Personalization through Query Expansion using the user's personal information repository. We use the data stored on the user's desktop to automatically expand the user query for providing personalized search results. Section 3.4 presents additional applications of the approaches, i.e. recommending related Web pages to the active task of the user in a Just-In-Time-IR fashion. A discussion in Section 3.5 gives a brief overview of the results achieved.

In Chapter 4 we present different approaches for performing automatic Semantic Enrichment. Section 4.1 introduces the topic and Section 4.2 presents a through analysis of tag usage across different types of tags for several Web 2.0 domains: Web sites, photos, and music. Using the finding of the analysis, we overcome the shortcomings by automatically generating annotations of underrepresented tags – tags not employed as annotations, but used in searches. In Section 4.3 we generate mood and theme annotations for music resources as well as emotion annotations for pictures. Section 4.4 presents approaches to annotate pictures with the events they have been taken at, and thus enabling fully automatic organization of resources into particular events as well as event categories. Next, a discussion in Section 4.5 summarizes the findings in the area of Semantic Enrichment.

Chapter 5 concludes the thesis with an enumeration of the contributions we brought to Information Retrieval research, while also discussing possible future research directions and open challenges associated to these topics.

2

Web IR: Background and Related Work

The World Wide Web ("WWW" or simply the "Web") is a global information medium which users can read and write via computers connected to the Internet. The history of the Internet dates back significantly further than that of the World Wide Web. As the amount of information grew exponentially, the need to retrieve specific information arose, such that different Information Retrieval methods were developed. IR is still evolving in present times, going from simple textual IR, over multimedia IR, over to different representations of the retrieved information, like event based or entity based visualizations.

Throughout the several next sections, we will present an overview of how the Internet and the Web were created, how IR started and continues to evolve using the services provided by the Web. We will emphasize different Web IR areas, with their specific challenges addressed in this thesis and related work.

2.1 History of the WWW and IR

In 1957 the USSR launches Sputnik, the first artificial earth satellite. In response, the United States forms the Advanced Research Projects Agency (ARPA) within the Department of Defense (DoD) to establish US lead in science and technology applicable to the military. During the Cold War and out of the need of having good control over missiles and bombers, in 1962 Paul Baran, commissioned by the US Air Force proposed a packet switched network as an underlying transport layer. The first physical network was constructed in 1969, linking four nodes: University of California at Los Angeles, SRI (in Stanford), University of California at Santa Barbara, and University of Utah. The network was wired together via 50 Kbps circuits. Development began in 1973 on the protocol later to be called TCP/IP, it was developed by a group headed by Vinton Cerf from Stanford and Bob Kahn from DARPA. This new protocol was to allow diverse computer networks to interconnect and communicate with each other. Vinton Cerf and Bob Kahn made first use of the term "Internet" in their paper on Transmission Control Protocol in 1974. Several developments followed like: Ethernet, UUCP, USENET, standardization of TCP/IP, DNS, deployment of T1 and T3 lines, etc. In 1990 Tim Berners-Lee and CERN in Geneva implement a hypertext system to provide efficient information access to the members of the international high-energy physics community, and the World-Wide Web was released by CERN in 1992.

Information Retrieval (IR) is the science of searching for documents, for information within documents, and for metadata about documents, as well as that of searching relational databases and the World Wide Web. Although Web search engines are the most visible IR applications and the verb "googleing" emerged, the history of IR goes over 65 years back. The idea of using computers to search for relevant pieces of information was popularized in the article "As We May Think"[Bus45] by Vannevar Bush in 1945. The first automated information retrieval systems were introduced in the 1950s and 1960s. By 1970 several different techniques had been shown to perform well on small text corpora such as the Cranfield collection (several thousand documents). Large-scale retrieval systems, such as the Lockheed Dialog system, came into use early in the 1970s.

In 1992 the US Department of Defense, along with the National Institute of Standards and Technology (NIST), cosponsored the Text Retrieval Conference (TREC) as part of the TIPSTER text program. The aim of this was to look into the information retrieval community by supplying the infrastructure that was needed for evaluation of text retrieval methodologies on a very large text collection. This catalyzed research on methods that scale to huge corpora. The introduction of Web search engines has boosted the need for very large scale retrieval systems even further.

2.2 Textual Information Retrieval

During the 1990s, studies showed that personal communication was the main means for information exchange, and people ignored the already existing IR systems. IR did not begin with the Web. In response to various challenges of providing information access, the field of IR evolved to give principled approaches to searching different forms of content, from scientific publications, over library records, to providing access to knowledge for professionals like lawyers, journalists, or doctors. However, with the exponential growth of the Web and the information within, along with optimizations in IR systems, people turned more and more toward (Web) IR systems for gathering information. Nowadays, Web IR has become a standard way to access information, being even faster and more convenient than asking colleagues or friends, and even preferred to looking through a pile of printed documents which is known to contain the desired answers.

An excellent introduction to IR is given by Manning, Raghavan and Schütze in

2.2 Textual Information Retrieval

[MRS08], where the definition to IR is given as: "Information Retrieval (IR) is finding material (usually documents) of an unstructured nature (usually text) that satisfies an information need from within large collections (usually stored on computers)." This section focuses on IR from textual documents; other types of IR (multimedia IR, event based IR, entity retrieval) are presented later on.

An IR process begins when a user enters a query into the system. Queries are formal statements of information needs, for example search strings in Web search engines. In information retrieval a query does not uniquely identify a single object in the collection. Instead, several objects may match the query, perhaps with different degrees of relevancy.

Several steps are needed in order to enable an efficient IR system, both at indexing and querying time:

- At indexing time:
  1. *collect* documents to be indexed (e.g. Web crawling)
  2. *tokenize* the documents into terms
  3. apply *stopword* removal (i.e. remove very common words, like "the", "of")
  4. *analyze*/normalize the tokens (e.g. lowercase, apply *stemming*)
  5. create an inverted *index*

- At querying time:
  1. preprocess the query similar to a document (i.e. tokenize, remove stopwords, analyze)
  2. match the query terms in the inverted index to retrieve matching documents
  3. rank the retrieved documents according to some criteria (e.g. $TFxIDF$, date)

We will explain the non-trivial steps in more detail below.

2.2.1 Inverted Index Structure

The way to avoid linearly scanning the texts for each query is to *index* the documents in advance. Similar to the index in a printed manual, the basic idea of an inverted index is shown in Table 2.1. For each term (making up a dictionary) in the document collection, a list (posting list) records which documents the term appears in. In practice, more complex structures are employed. They contain the *Document Frequency* (DF) – the total number of documents a term appears in – along with the term in the dictionary. The posting list also contains for each document the *Term Frequency*

(TF) – the number of occurrences of the term in that particular document –, and also the positions at which the term appears in the document. Ranking of documents in response to a query can only be made possible by using these additional statistics (discussed below), and term positions enable queries like "a *near* b" or phrase queries.

Terms (Dictionary)	Documents (Posting Lists)
hello	$document_1, document_5, document_{27}$
the	$document_1, document_2, document_3, document_5, document_6, ...$
world	$document_{17}, document_{18}$
...	...

Table 2.1 Basic inverted index structure

The index has to be built once (with updates on changes), and it enables very fast document retrieval, even for complex queries. In case of a one-term query, the list of retrieved documents is the posting list itself. For complex multi-term queries several posting lists (for the different sought terms) are combined; AND operators result in an intersection, OR results in union, and NOT in returning all documents except the ones in the posting list. Different query optimization and caching techniques are employed additionally.

2.2.2 Ranking and *TFxIDF* Weighting

Documents are represented in the *bag of words* model: each document consists of a set of terms, where the exact ordering of the terms in the text is ignored; only the number of occurrences is retained. This means that in classical IR "the fox jumps over the dog" is the same as "the dog jumps over the fox". The Term Frequency (TF) of a term in a document – denoted $tf_{t,d}$ – is the number of occurrences of the term in a given document. The Document Frequency (DF) on the other hand denotes the number of documents in the collection that contain the term t – df_t. In order to scale the weight of a term, the Inverse Document Frequency (IDF) is used, with $idf_t = log\frac{N}{df_t}$, where N is the total number of documents in the collection.

Thus the $tf_{t,d}$ is higher as the document d discusses term t more, and idf is higher for rare terms and lower for more frequent terms in the collection. To produce a composite weight for each term in each document, a combination of TF and IDF is created: $tfidf_{t,d} = tf_{t,d} \cdot idf_t$.

We can see each document as a vector with one component corresponding to each term in the dictionary ($\vec{V}(d)$), together with a weight for each component that is given by the $tfidf$ score. The representation of a set of documents as vectors in a common vector space is known as the *vector space model* and is fundamental to a host of IR operations including scoring documents for a given query. Therefore, to quantify the

2.2 Textual Information Retrieval

similarity between two documents (where one of the documents can actually be the query) we compute the *cosine similarity* of their vector representations $\vec{V}(d_1)$ and $\vec{V}(d_2)$:

$$sim(d_1, d_2) = \frac{\vec{V}(d_1) \cdot \vec{V}(d_2)}{|\vec{V}(d_1)||\vec{V}(d_2)|} \qquad (2.1)$$

Several modifications and normalizations can be applied to TF and IDF, e.g. logarithm, as seen in Figure 2.1. The output of an IR system for a query q will be then a list of documents matching q, and ranked by $sim(d_i, q)$ for each d_i in the retrieved results. Depending on the implementation of the IR system, different optimizations are made in order to efficiently compute the ranking over large collections of documents.

term frequency		document frequency		normalization	
n (natural)	$tf_{t,d}$	n (no)	1	n (none)	1
l (logarithm)	$1 + \log(tf_{t,d})$	t (idf)	$\log \frac{N}{df_t}$	c (cosine)	$\frac{1}{\sqrt{w_1^2 + w_2^2 + \ldots + w_M^2}}$
a (augmented)	$0.5 + \frac{0.5 \times tf_{t,d}}{\max_t(tf_{t,d})}$	p (prob idf)	$\max(0, \log \frac{N - df_t}{df_t})$	u (pivoted unique)	$1/u$
b (boolean)	$\begin{cases} 1 \text{ if } tf_{t,d} > 0 \\ 0 \text{ otherwise} \end{cases}$			b (byte size)	$1/CharLength^\alpha, \alpha < 1$
L (log ave)	$\frac{1 + \log(tf_{t,d})}{1 + \log(ave_{t \in d}(tf_{t,d}))}$				

Figure 2.1 SMART notation for *tfidf* variants, as in [MRS08]

2.2.3 Evaluation Metrics

Many different measures for evaluating the performance of IR systems have been proposed. The measures require a collection of documents and a query. All common measures described here assume a ground truth notion of relevancy: every document is known to be either relevant or non-relevant to a particular query. In practice queries may be ill-posed and there may be different shades of relevancy.

Precision. Precision is the fraction of the documents retrieved that are relevant to the user's information need.

$$precision = \frac{|\{relevant\ documents\} \cap \{retrieved\ documents\}|}{|\{retrieved\ documents\}|} \qquad (2.2)$$

In binary classification, precision is analogous to positive predictive value.

P@n. Precision takes all retrieved documents into account. It can also be evaluated at a given cut-off rank, considering only the topmost results returned by the system. This measure is called precision at n or P@n. For example, P@10 represents the precision value for the first 10 retrieved results.

R-Precision. Analogous to P@n, R-Precision is the precision value for the first R results, where R is the number of relevant results.

Recall Recall is the fraction of the documents that are relevant to the query that are successfully retrieved.

$$recall = \frac{|\{relevant\ documents\} \cap \{retrieved\ documents\}|}{|\{relevant\ documents\}|} \quad (2.3)$$

In binary classification, recall is called sensitivity. So it can be looked at as the probability that a relevant document is retrieved by the query. It is trivial to achieve recall of 100% by returning all documents in response to any query. Therefore recall alone is not enough but one needs to measure the number of non-relevant documents also, for example by computing the precision.

F-Measure. The weighted harmonic mean of precision and recall, the traditional F-measure or balanced F-score is:

$$F = \frac{2 \cdot precision \cdot recall}{precision + recall} \quad (2.4)$$

This is also known as the F_1 measure, because recall and precision are evenly weighted. The general formula for non-negative real β is:

$$F_\beta = \frac{(1+\beta^2) \cdot precision \cdot recall}{\beta^2 \cdot precision + recall} \quad (2.5)$$

Two other commonly used F measures are the F_2 measure, which weights recall twice as much as precision, and the $F_{0.5}$ measure, which weights precision twice as much as recall.

MAP. Mean Average Precision is computed as:

$$MAP = \frac{1}{|Q|} \sum_{i=1}^{|Q|} AP_i, \quad (2.6)$$

where $|Q|$ is the number of queries and AP is obtained averaging the Precision values calculated at each rank where a relevant entity is retrieved [BYRN99]:

$$AP = \frac{1}{|Rel|} \sum_{i=1}^{|Rel|} \frac{i}{rank(i)}, \quad (2.7)$$

where $rank(i)$ is the rank of the i-th relevant result, and $|Rel|$ is the number of relevant results. A score of 0 is assumed for any not-retrieved relevant entities.

NDCG. Discounted Cumulative Gain (DCG) [JK00] is a rich measure, as it gives more weight to highly ranked documents, while also incorporating different relevance levels by giving them different gain values:

$$DCG(i) = \begin{cases} G(1) & ,if\ i=1 \\ DCG(i-1) + G(i)/log(i) & ,otherwise. \end{cases}$$

NDCG normalizes the DCG value by the maximum achievable value.

MRR. Mean Reciprocal Rank is a statistic for evaluating any process that produces a list of possible responses to a query, ordered by probability of correctness. The reciprocal rank of a query response is the multiplicative inverse of the rank of the first correct answer. The mean reciprocal rank is the average of the reciprocal ranks of results for a sample of queries Q:

$$MRR = \frac{1}{|Q|} \sum_{i=1}^{|Q|} \frac{1}{rank_i} \qquad (2.8)$$

2.3 Search Personalization

Standard IR systems have the drawback that they do not differentiate between different kinds of users, which might have different information needs expressed by identical queries. The IR system will return the same result list for a reporter and a tourist when issuing a query like "Brazil events", although one is interested in political events and the other in entertainment. Search Personalization addresses this issue and tries to add background information about the user to the query. In this section we present work that has been done in different areas of search personalization. We also address this issue in Chapter 3 as well as in the following publications: [FNP07, CFN07, BCFN07, CFN06b, GCC+08, PFN08, CFN06a].

We will present related work from two IR areas: Search Personalization (Section 2.3.1) and Automatic Query Expansion (Section 2.3.2). There exists a vast amount of algorithms for both domains. However, not much has been done specifically aimed at combining them. We thus present a separate analysis, first introducing some approaches to personalize search, as this represents the main goal of our research, and then discussing several query expansion techniques and their relationship to our algorithms. Relevant work also includes Just-In-Time IR agents (JITIRs) (Section 2.3.3) and summarization algorithms (Section 2.3.4).

Only few publications combine these areas and even fewer address both the PC Desktop and the World Wide Web. The work of Teevan et al. [TDH05] is the only one exploiting desktop data for web search. They modified the query term weights from the BM25 weighting scheme [JWR98] to incorporate user interests as captured by the desktop index, which is related to our approach. However, they select their web search query based on explicitly user entered keywords which they refine using expansion terms from the Top-K documents returned by the web search engine, whereas we use an *automatically* generated query from user's currently active document.

2.3.1 Personalized Search

Personalized search comprises two major components: (1) User profiles, and (2) The actual search algorithm. This section splits the relevant background according to the focus of each article into either one of these elements.

Approaches focused on the User Profile. Sugiyama et al. [SHY04] analyzed surfing behavior and generated user profiles as features (terms) of the visited pages. Upon issuing a new query, the search results were ranked based on the similarity between each URL and the user profile. Qiu and Cho [QC06] used Machine Learning on the past click history of the user in order to determine topic preference vectors and then apply Topic-Sensitive PageRank [Hav02]. User profiling based on browsing history has the advantage of being rather easy to obtain and process. This is probably why it is also employed by several industrial search engines (e.g., Yahoo! MyWeb[1]). However, it is definitely not sufficient for gathering a thorough insight into user's interests. More, it requires to store all personal information at the server side, which raises significant privacy concerns.

Only two other approaches enhanced Web search using Desktop data, yet both used different core ideas: (1) Teevan et al. [TDH05] modified the query *term weights* from the BM25 weighting scheme to incorporate user interests as captured by their Desktop indexes; (2) In Chirita et al. [CFN06a], we focused on *re-ranking* the Web search output according to the cosine distance between each URL and a set of Desktop terms describing user's interests. Moreover, none of these investigated the adaptive application of personalization.

Approaches focused on the Personalization Algorithm. Effectively building the personalization aspect directly into PageRank [PBMW98] (i.e., by biasing it on a target set of pages) has received much attention recently. Havelimala [Hav02] computed a topic-oriented PageRank, in which 16 PageRank vectors biased on each of the main topics of the Open Directory were initially calculated off-line, and then combined at run-time based on the similarity between the user query and each of the 16 topics. More recently, Nie et al. [NDQ06] modified the idea by distributing the PageRank of a page across the topics it contains in order to generate topic oriented rankings. Jeh and Widom [JW03] proposed an algorithm that avoids the massive resources needed for storing one Personalized PageRank Vector (PPV) per user by precomputing PPVs only for a small set of pages and then applying linear combination. As the computation of PPVs for larger sets of pages was still quite expensive, several solutions have been investigated, the most important ones being those of Fogaras and Racz [FR05], and Sarlos et al. [SBC+06], the latter using rounding and count-min sketching in order to fastly obtain accurate enough approximations of the personalized scores.

2.3.2 Automatic Query Expansion

Automatic query expansion aims at deriving a better formulation of the user query in order to enhance retrieval. It is based on exploiting various social or collection

---

[1] http://myWeb2.search.yahoo.com

2.3 Search Personalization

specific characteristics in order to generate additional terms, which are appended to the original input keywords before identifying the matching documents returned as output. In this section we survey some of the representative query expansion works grouped according to the source employed to generate additional terms: (1) Relevance feedback, (2) Collection based co-occurrence statistics, and (3) Thesaurus information. Some other approaches are also addressed in the end of the section.

Relevance Feedback Techniques. The main idea of Relevance Feedback (RF) is that useful information can be extracted from the relevant documents returned for the initial query. First approaches were manual [Roc71] in the sense that the user was the one choosing the relevant results, and then various methods were applied to extract new terms, related to the query and the selected documents. Efthimiadis [Eft95] presented a comprehensive literature review and proposed several simple methods to extract such new keywords based on term frequency, document frequency, etc. We used some of these as inspiration for our Desktop specific techniques. Chang and Hsu [CH98] asked users to choose relevant clusters, instead of documents, thus reducing the amount of interaction necessary. RF has also been shown to be effectively automatized by considering the top ranked documents as relevant [XC96] (this is known as Pseudo RF). Lam and Jones [LAJ01] used summarization to extract informative sentences from the top-ranked documents, and appended them to the user query. Carpineto et al. [CdMRB01] maximized the divergence between the language model defined by the top retrieved documents and that defined by the entire collection. Finally, Yu et al. [YCWM03] selected the expansion terms from vision-based segments of Web pages in order to cope with the multiple topics residing therein.

Co-occurrence Based Techniques. Terms highly co-occurring with the issued keywords have been shown to increase precision when appended to the query [KC99]. Many statistical measures have been developed to best assess "term relationship" levels, either analyzing entire documents [QF93], lexical affinity relationships [CFPS02] (i.e., pairs of closely related words which contain exactly one of the initial query terms), etc. We have also investigated three such approaches in order to identify query relevant keywords from the rich, yet rather complex Personal Information Repository.

Thesaurus Based Techniques. A broadly explored method is to expand the user query with new terms, whose meaning is closely related to the input keywords. Such relationships are usually extracted from large scale thesauri, as WordNet [Mil95], in which various sets of synonyms, hypernyms, etc. are predefined. Just as for the co-occurrence methods, initial experiments with this approach were controversial, either reporting improvements, or even reductions in output quality [Voo94]. Recently, as the experimental collections grew larger, and as the employed algorithms became more complex, better results have been obtained [SC04, KSR04, LLYM04]. We also use WordNet based expansion terms. However, we base this process on analyzing the Desktop level relationship between the original query and the proposed new keywords.

Other Techniques. There are many other attempts to extract expansion terms.

Though orthogonal to our approach, two works are very relevant for the Web environment: Cui et al. [CWNM02] generated word correlations utilizing the probability for query terms to appear in each document, as computed over the search engine logs. Kraft and Zien [KZ04] showed that anchor text is very similar to user queries, and thus exploited it to acquire additional keywords.

2.3.3 Just-in-Time Information Retrieval

Rhodes and Maes [RM00] describe a new class of software agents, that of Just-in-Time Information Retrieval Agents (JITIRs), which are software agents that proactively present potentially valuable information based on a person's local context in an easily accessible yet non-intrusive manner. JITIRs provide useful or supporting information that is relevant to the current task, research results demonstrate that such systems encourage use of information that would not otherwise be looked at. Rhodes presents the kinds of agents: (1) The Remembrance Agent [RS96], an agent incorporated in Emacs, which continually presents a list of documents, from the PC desktop or from various databases, that are related to the current document being written or read. (2) Margin Notes [Rho00] is a JITIR agent that automatically rewrites web pages as they are loaded into the browser adding hyperlinks to personal files, each HTML section receiving its own annotation in addition to a general entire page annotation. (3) Jimminy [Rho97] is a third type of JITIR agent that provides information based on a person's physical environment. By using a shoulder-mounted wearable computer containing different environment-aware sensors, suggestions are presented to the user on an head-mounted display. All three JITIR agents presented by Rhodes use the same back-end system, called Savant, which computes the relevance score for each annotation based on co-occurrence of words using a term frequency / inverse-document frequency ($TFIDF$) method [Sal88] and the Okapi weighting scheme [WRB$^+$98]. The power of Savant comes from a strong template matching system that recognizes document structures and parses different fields. As necessary features of a JITIR agent, Rhodes [RM00] lists proactivity, the presentation of information in an accessible yet non-intrusive manner, and awareness of the user's local context.

Budzik and Hammond [BH99] introduced the concept of Information Management Assistants (IMAs). IMAs automatically discover related material on behalf of the user by serving as an intelligent intermediary between the user and information retrieval systems. Budzik et al.'s Watson system runs in the background on a user's computer and when possible retrieves web links similar to the active web page in the browser (Microsoft Internet Explorer or Mozilla FireFox), Microsoft Word, or Microsoft Outlook. These links are retrieved using different information sources like AltaVista Web Search and other user definable repositories, and are then presented in a separate window after a simple URL and page title based clustering is applied. For Watson, weighting terms in order to form a search query is highly dependent on a document's internal layout and word highlighting. In addition to document

2.3 Search Personalization

specific heuristics, Watson uses a standard information retrieval $TFIDF$ weighting scheme after removing stop words, combined with word position information in the given document. In addition, Watson allows users to enter explicit queries, which are then refined by means of context related information extracted from the active document. In subsequent work [BHBK00], Budzik et al. argue about the usefulness of the retrieved results, stating that an IMA should focus on retrieving not only similar documents but documents that are relevant and useful in purposeful and interesting ways. In their experiments they assess that the similarity of a result accounts for about a quarter of the variance in the utility of a result.

Other JITIRs include Letizia [Lie95], an agent which creates a short term user profile by compiling keywords contained in visited web pages, and highlights outgoing links from the current web page that match the profile. WebWatcher [JFM97] is a system similar to Letizia, highlighting hyperlinks that match a user's stated interest. Maglio et al.'s SUITOR [MBCS00] uses multiple agents to watch several applications in parallel and provide results for the overall activity. RADAR [CST98] is a different front end for the Remenbrance Agent [RS96] described earlier that uses Microsoft Word instead of Emacs and displays suggestions in a separate window, with Savant as information-retrieval engine. Finally, there are domain-specific JITIR agents like The Peace, Love, and Understanding Machine (PLUM) system [Elo95] which adds hyperlinks to disaster news stories.

2.3.4 Summarization

Automated summarization deals with concatenating text-span excerpts (i.e., sentences, paragraphs, etc.) into a human understandable document summary, it dates back to the 1950's [Luh58]. With the advent of the World Wide Web and large scale search engines, increased attention has been focused towards this research area and several new approaches have been proposed. The diversity of concepts covered by a document was first explored by Carbonell and Goldstein [CG98]. They proposed using Maximal Marginal Relevance (MMR), which selects summary sentences that are both relevant to the user query and least similar to the previously chosen ones. Later, Nomoto and Matsumoto [NM01] developed this into a generic single-document summarizer that first identifies the topics within the input text, and then outputs the most important sentence of each topic area.

Another approach is to generate the summary as the set of top ranked sentences from the original document according to their salience or likelihood of being part of a summary [GKMC99, ER04]. Consequently, more search specific applications of summarization have been proposed. Zeng et al. [ZHC$^+$04] used extraction and ranking of salient phrases when clustering web search results. Others have used hierarchies to improve user access to search output by summarizing and categorizing retrieved documents [LC03], or to organize topic words extracted from textual documents [LCR01, SC99].

2.4 Web 2.0 and Multimedia IR

The term "Web 2.0" is commonly associated with web applications that facilitate interactive information sharing, interoperability, user-centered design, and collaboration on the World Wide Web. A Web 2.0 site allows its users to interact with each other as contributors to the website's content, in contrast to websites where users are limited to the passive viewing of information that is provided to them. Examples of Web 2.0 include Web-based communities, hosted services, Web applications, social-networking sites, video-sharing sites, wikis, blogs, mashups, and folksonomies.

The term is closely associated with Tim O'Reilly because of the O'Reilly Media Web 2.0 conference in 2004. Although the term suggests a new version of the World Wide Web, it does not refer to an update to any technical specifications, but rather to cumulative changes in the ways software developers and end-users use the Web. Whether Web 2.0 is qualitatively different from prior Web technologies has been challenged by World Wide Web inventor Tim Berners-Lee, who called the term a "piece of jargon" – precisely because he specifically intended the Web to embody these values in the first place.

Web 2.0 websites allow users to do more than just retrieve information. They can build on the interactive facilities of "Web 1.0" to provide "Network as platform" computing, allowing users to run software applications entirely through a browser. Users can own the data on a Web 2.0 site and exercise control over that data. These sites may have an architecture of participation that encourages users to add value to the application as they use it.

The impossibility of excluding group members who do not contribute to the provision of goods from sharing profits gives rise to the possibility that rational members will prefer to withhold their contribution of effort and free-ride on the contribution of others. This requires what is sometimes called Radical Trust by the management of the website. The characteristics of Web 2.0 are: rich user experience, user participation, dynamic content, metadata, web standards and scalability. Further characteristics, such as openness, freedom and collective intelligence by way of user participation, can also be viewed as essential attributes of Web 2.0.

The most prominent characteristic of Web 2.0 is *tagging* – assigning short textual descriptions (most commonly one word) to describe resources. Tags are added by individuals for the purpose of self-organization; nevertheless, when aggregating tags over enough users for one resource, an accurate description of that resource is provided. As an example consider the aggregation of the most used tags when relating to Web 2.0 in Figure 2.2.

2.4.1 Social Web Sites

Web 2.0 enables information sharing, collaboration among users and most notably supports active participation and creativity of the users. We present a list of the

2.4 Web 2.0 and Multimedia IR

Figure 2.2 Tag cloud presenting Web 2.0 themes

most noticeable social sites on the Web, along with a short description. The number of sites providing Web 2.0 functionality is still growing, and most of the once static sites try to incorporate also Web 2.0 capabilities.

- *Del.icio.us* – http://www.delicious.com/ – The premiere social bookmarking Web site for storing, sharing, and discovering Web bookmarks, where users can tag each of their bookmarks with freely chosen keywords. A combined view of everyones bookmarks with a given tag is available and users can view bookmarks added by similar-minded users.

- *Flickr* – http://www.flickr.com/ – One of the earliest Web 2.0 applications; it is currently the most popular photo sharing website and online community platform. *Flickr* asks photo submitters to describe images using tags, to allow searchers to (re-)find pictures using place name, subject matter, or other aspects of the picture.

- *Picasa* – http://picasa.google.com/ – A desktop photo viewing and organization application, as well as a Web photo sharing application are provided by *Picasa* to integrate and ease publishing of photos from the personal collections.

- *YouTube* – http://www.youtube.com/ – *YouTube* is a video-sharing website on which users can upload, share, and view videos. It uses Flash video technology to display a wide variety of user-generated video content, including movie clips, TV clips, and music videos, as well as amateur content such as video blogging and short original videos.

- *Last.fm* – http://www.last.fm/ – For the music domain, *Last.fm* is the worlds largest social music platform, with over 20 million active users based in more than 230 countries. Since August 2005, *Last.fm* supports tagging of artists, albums, and tracks to create a site-wide folksonomy of music.

- *AllMusic.com* – http://www.allmusic.com/ – The content is created by professional data entry staff, editors, and writers. The network of writers includes over 9000 music critics who review albums and songs and write artist biographies. *AllMusic.com* claims to have the largest digital archive of music, including about six million digital songs, as well as the largest cover art library, with more than half a million cover image scans.

- *Digg* – http://www.digg.com/ – A social news website. The site's cornerstone function consists of letting people vote stories up or down, called digging and burying, respectively. Many stories get submitted every day, but only the most Dugg stories appear on the front page. *Digg*'s popularity has prompted the creation of other social networking sites with story submission and voting systems.

- *StumbleUpon* – http://www.stumbleupon.com/ – An Internet community that allows its users to discover and rate Web pages, photos, and videos. It is a personalized recommendation engine which uses peer and social-networking principles. Web pages are presented when the user clicks the "Stumble!" button on the browser's toolbar.

- *Facebook* – http://www.facebook.com/ – Facebook is a social networking website launched in February 2004 and operated and privately owned by Facebook, Inc.[1] Users can add people as friends and send them messages, and update their personal profiles to notify friends about themselves. Additionally, users can join networks organized by workplace, school, or college.

- *MySpace* – http://www.myspace.com/ – A social networking website, similar to *Facebook*, where people can link to friends, share photos and videos, and send messages to each other. *MySpace* became the most popular social networking site in the United States in June 2006. *MySpace* was overtaken internationally by its main competitor, *Facebook*, in April 2008, based on monthly unique visitors.

Several social systems have been acquired by search engine companies *Flickr* and *Del.icio.us* by Yahoo!, *YouTube* and *Picasa* by Google – which now also extend search to these communities.

2.4.2 Multimedia IR Using Textual Annotations

Today, with the most prominent search engines on the Web users are still constrained to search for multimedia resources using textual queries. E.g. tags and other metadata (e.g. extracted from ID3 tags), can be indexed together and later be used to support music search.

In recent years, collaborative tagging has become extremely popular among users – they associate descriptive keywords to various types of content (e.g. pictures, Web pages, publications, movies and music). As short textual descriptions, tags are useful for content organization or for supporting search and retrieval. As a result, a huge amount of manually created metadata describing all kinds of resources is now available. While for Web pages or publications, tags may not improve retrieval that much, as most of the tags can also be found in the textual representation of these documents (see [HRGM08]), for pictures, music or movies the gain is substantial. Content-based retrieval is still not mature enough to enable scalable content-based search, so tags can nicely be used for enhancement of metadata indexes in digital libraries. Supporting users in the process of tagging resources should therefore be strongly encouraged.

One possibility to make users use keywords from the categories we need is to unobtrusively recommend such tags and thus support the users in the tagging process. Besides minimizing cognitive load by changing the task from generation to recognition [SOHB07] such recommendation of under-represented but valuable tags will very likely trigger reinforcement, i.e. enforce preferential attachment. As presented in [SLR+06, HRS07], seeing previous tag assignments from other users strongly influences which tags will be assigned next and thus to which tag set a resource's vocabulary will converge.

2.5 Tags as User Generated Content

Given that Web 2.0 tools and platforms have made collaborative tagging highly popular, some studies have started to investigate tagging motivations and patterns, but they are usually focusing on one specific collection only [GH06, HRS07, SLR+06, AN07, HKGM08] or provide first qualitative insights across collections from very small samples [MNBD06, Zol07]. We will shortly review some of the major work related to the areas we also address in Section 4.2: tagging behavior, as well as search and knowledge discovery based on social tags. Later, in Chapter 4 (as well as in the following publications: [BFNP10, FGNP10, BFK+09, BFP+09b, BFNP09, BFP09a, BFNP08]), we overcome some of the challenges in this area.

2.5.1 Tag Analyses

Tag Types. First analyses of tagging systems show that the reasons for tagging are diverse and with them the kinds of tags used. Marlow et al. [MNBD06] identifies organizational motivations for tagging, as well as social tagging motivations, such as opinion expression, the attraction of attention, and self-presentation [GH06, MNBD06] or providing context to friends [AN07]. The different tag types shed light on what distinctions are important to taggers [GH06]. According to [Zol07], in free-for-all systems opinion expression, self-presentation, activism and performance tags become more frequent, while in self-tagging systems like *Flickr* or *Del.icio.us* users tag almost exclusively for their own benefit of enhanced information organization [GH06]. Sen et al. [SLR+06] showed in an experiment on vocabulary formation in the MovieLens system how different design choices affect the nature/types of tags used, their distributions and the convergence within a group, i.e. the proportions that "Factual", "Subjective" and "Personal" tags will have.

Tags Supporting Search. Based on the idea that tags in bookmarking systems usually provide good summaries of the resources and that they indicate the popularity of a page, Bao et al. [BWF+07] investigated the use of tags for improving Web search. The proposed SocialSimilarityRank measures the association between tags and SocialPageRank accounts for the popularity among taggers in terms of a frequency ranking. In [HJSS06], the authors suggest an adapted PageRank-like algorithm, FolkRank, to improve efficient searching via personalized and topic-specific ranking within the tag space. This can be used to recommend interesting users, resources and related tags to increase the chance of "serendipitous encounters". In music retrieval, tags can be used as an alternative or additional possibility to find songs: In [FNP07], *Last.fm* songs are not only recommended based on track-lists (song and artist) of similar users, but also by considering (descriptive) tags. Here, tag-based search algorithms provide better and faster recommendation results than traditional track-based collaborative filtering methods.

In [HKGM08], the authors try to answer the question whether social bookmarking data can be used to augment Web search. Their analysis of a *Del.icio.us* dataset shows that tags tend to gravitate toward certain domains and that tags occur in over 50% of the resources they annotate, thus potentially improving search. Even if the usefulness of tags has been proven at a single-site level, some general study of the types of tags used inside multiple systems and their general implications for search is still missing. In Section 4.2 we tackle this aspect and perform an in-depth analysis over three different systems.

2.5.2 Knowledge Discovery Through Tags

Knowledge Discovery for Music. While automatic identification of music themes has not been studied so far, several works in Music Information Retrieval have shown a potential to model the mood from audio content. For example, [LLZ03] relies on extracted low level features like timbre, intensity and rhythm (modeled in a Gaussian Mixture Model) to classify music according to Thayer's model of emotions [Tha89]. Similarly, in [FZP03] the authors propose a schema such that music databases are indexed on four labels of music mood: "happiness", "sadness", "anger" and "fear". An important limitation of these approaches is that they can not capture other 'external' sources of emotionality, for example, events that people may associate with a certain piece of music. [ELBMG07] investigate social tags for improving music recommendations to attenuate the cold-start problem by automatically predicting additional tags based on the learned relationship between existing tags and acoustic features. In [CWN09], *Last.fm* user tags have been used together with content-based features for automatic genre classification. Underlining the usefulness of social tags for music classification, Levy and Sandler [LS07] found that *Last.fm* tags define a low-dimensional semantic space which is able to effectively capture sensible attributes as well as music similarity. Especially at the track level this space is highly organized by artist and genre.

Knowledge Discovery for Pictures. Picture metadata enrichment is similar to music metadata enrichment in that the goal can be achieved by either using information inferred from the low level features of the resources, or from already provided user annotations. In [AHS06], user tags are combined with content-based techniques in order to improve data navigation and search: A classifier uses low-level features, like color and texture, in addition to tags provided by the users in order to discover new relationships between data. ZoneTag[2] [NN08] automatically recommends location tags for photos taken with a mobile phone, based on the phone's position. In [SvZ08], the authors focus on a subset of *Flickr* pictures and analyze the different tag categories used by users to annotate their pictures. The analysis is performed automatically based on WordNet categories. The paper also tackles the aspect of tag recommendation.

Rattenbury et al. [RGN07] try to extract event and place semantics from tags assigned to photos in *Flickr* relying on burst analysis. In [ACN$^+$09], landmark pictures for city sights are identified accompanied by representative tags by employing machine learning based on the user generated tags in *Flickr*. Investigating tag evolution in *Flickr*, Dubinko et al. [DKM$^+$06] developed algorithms to find the most interesting tags to be displayed in Flash animations. Predicting moods/emotions for pictures is much less popular than for music. Prior work uses content-based methods to analyze and classify facial expressions (see [FL03] for an overview), sometimes also picture mood independent of peoples' faces [DNBL08]. In contrast to prior work, our algorithms can distinguish a much richer set of emotions/moods than the often very simple models underlying content-based approaches.

2.5.3 Tagging Motivations and Types of Tags

Analyses of collaborative tagging systems indicate that incentives for tagging are quite manifold and so are the kinds of tags used. According to [MNBD06], organizational motivations for enhanced information access and sharing are predominant, though also social motivations can be encountered, such as opinion expression, attraction of attention, self-presentation [MNBD06, GH06].Which of those incentives is most

---
[2]http://zonetag.research.yahoo.com

characteristic for a particular system seems to vary, depending on tagging rights, tagging support, aggregation model, etc.– all influencing why certain kinds of tags are used. [GH06] and [Zol07] indicate that in free-for-all tagging systems like *Last.fm*, opinion expression, self-presentation, activism and performance tags become frequent, while in self-tagging systems like *Flickr* or *Del.icio.us* users tag almost exclusively for their own benefit of enhanced information organization.

Despite the different motivations and behaviors, stable structures do emerge in collaborative tagging systems [GH06, HRS07, HJSS06]. The evolving patterns follow a scale-free power law distribution, indicating convergence of the vocabulary to a set of very frequent words, coexisting with a long tail of rarely used terms [HRS07, HJSS06]. Studying the evolution of tagging vocabularies in the MovieLens system, [SLR$^+$06] use controlled experiments with varying system features to prove how such design decisions heavily influence the convergence process within a group, i.e. the proportions "Factual", "Subjective" and "Personal" tags will have. According to these results, being able to display automatically identified "Factual" tags only would lead to even more factual and interpersonally useful tags. Similarly, in their paper on collaborative tag suggestions, [XFMS06] introduce a taxonomy of five classes: Content, Context, Attribute, Subjective and Organizational tags.

[BFNP08] introduce an empirically verified tag type taxonomy comprising eight categories (Topic, Time, Location, Type, Author/Owner, Opinions/Quality, Usage context, Self reference) that is applicable to any tagging system, not bound to any particular resource type. Besides establishing type distributions for *Last.fm*, *Del.icio.us* and *Flickr*, the authors discuss the potential of the different identified categories for supporting search. A complementing query log analysis showed that e.g. highly personal self-reference tags are indeed not used in querying a web search engine. Similarly, subjective usage context and opinions are rarely queried for, nor judged very useful for searching public web pages. Only for music these queries play an important role with people often searching for "wedding songs" or "party music". Here, interpersonal agreement seems higher due to the restricted domain and, probably, shared culture.

2.6 Event Based IR

We describe the world by using words. Yet, words usually bring to mind different mental views of the world for different individuals, because of their personal experience and context. This is the reason why the "semantic gap" between our conceptualizations of the world, expressed using language, and our experience of the world, whose most direct representations are media, is far beyond the reach of current systems. And it is also why, so far, a universal solution of the problem of contextualizing search, navigation, and media management in general to the user needs and the operating environment has not been found. Our lives are a constellation of events, which one

2.6 Event Based IR

after another, pace our everyday activities and build up our memories. The key idea underlying Event Based IR is to use events as the primary means to organize and index media, e.g., photos, videos, journal articles. Instead of starting from media and seeing, a posteriori, how we can meaningfully understand their contents (e.g., by tagging them), we organize a priori our data and knowledge in terms of events and use media to populate them, thus providing their experiential dimension. Events provide the common framework inside which the local experience-driven contextual information can be not only coded, but also shared and reduced to a common denominator. Events have both a local and a global dimension. The local dimension enables the mapping of tags (conceptualizations) to media (personal experiences), while the global dimension enables the sharing of event descriptions (thus enabling social sharing and networking of events, media, and tags) and event structures across similar events, thus providing a common way to index media (social sharing and networking of event structures). In turn, the networking of events and event structures enables the creation of networked communities inside which common (global) descriptions of the world can be built and continuously enriched by the continuous flow of individual (local) descriptions.

Image recognition is still largely an unsolved problem, and tagging media (e.g., photos) is still largely a manual process. The "semantic gap" between our conceptualizations of the world, expressed using language, and our experience of the world, whose most direct representations are photos and media in general, is far beyond the reach of current media understanding systems. Thus, content-based media search is still very much example-driven (e.g., find photos similar to a given one on the basis of a set of features). On the other hand, our life is a constellation of events; events such as a birthday, a marriage, a summer vacation, or a car accident are the lens through which we see and memorize our own personal experiences. In turn, global events, such as world sport championships or global natural disasters (e.g., the 2004 tsunami, climate change, or the world recession) or, on a smaller scale, a local festival or a soccer match, build collective experiences that allow us to share personal experiences as part of a more social phenomenon that we could call "collective events". When describing events, we ground in our experience our common and abstract understanding of the world and the language that we use to describe it. The generic notion of "beach" is then associated to a specific time and place, which is frozen in the photo or movie that we have taken.

2.6.1 Application Scenario

The shift from classical producer-consumer paradigm to the so-called prosumer, where users generate new multimedia content by capturing their own experience in images and videos, mixing it with digital material collected from the web, and finally sharing it with other users, highlights novel and highly challenging issues in networked media search and retrieval. Big media companies such as CNN or BBC welcome pictures, videos and reports from the audience in order to report from places where their reporters are not yet on the ground. Like this they can report very rapidly, or even in real time. Current TV created a new model for peer-to-peer news and information network, produced and programmed in collaboration with its audience. The popularity and data volume of modern social Web 2.0 content sharing applications originate in their ease of operation for even inexperienced users, suitable mechanisms for supporting collaboration, and attractiveness of shared annotated material about events (images in *Flickr*, videos in *YouTube*, bookmarks in *Del.icio.us*, etc.). The growing size and increasing number of folksonomies, blogs, news portals and personal repositories pose new challenges in terms of search and mining for relevant content and finding other users sharing the same interests. Ideally, sharing platforms should provide the user with adaptive browsing mechanisms and recommendations for potentially relevant content and annotation mechanisms for her personal event-related data.

To offer a viable solution to these problems, we will make reference to an application domain, which allows looking at the global picture from different complementary perspectives, thus achieving a comprehensive understanding of the relevant problems. Suppose, Carla Kolumna is a big fan of skiing. As the Olympic Games started recently in Vancouver, she is looking for events in the corresponding Olympic disciplines. Carla queries the user interface for the *Olympic Games* event. The result set contains the main event as well as a list of sub-events that can be browsed . She takes a look at the featured videos and then starts exploring the sub-event *Alpine Skiing* (which can also contain further sub-events). After having watched some interesting videos and pictures, she sees the list of related events shown in the interface: Ski Jumping, Biathlon, Cross Country, etc. She further explores *Ski Jumping* and being really impressed she decides to accept the system's recommendation to join a ski sports community. More specifically, she joins the community of Ski jumping fans Germany through which she has access to a lot of content about the performances of German ski jumpers. Carla gets really excited about the gold medal jump of K. Blaubär and wants to get a 3D impression and see photos of the jump from different angles and perspectives. As a result, she finds images uploaded from different spectators, i.e. different peoples' view points on the same event. Event IR can turn such a scenario into reality.

2.6.2 Event Detection

The first step towards efficient event based IR is detecting events from (multimedia or textual) data sources. Some work has been done on detecting events from textual information; event detection from extensive textual sources (i.e. Web size) or from Web 2.0 sources is still in an early stage. The topic of *event detection* is not new, first papers addressing this domain appeared already in 1998, as part of the *Topic Detection and Tracking (TDT)* initiative [APL98]. In [YPC98] the authors introduce

2.6 Event Based IR

two different types of event detection methods: retrospective and online detection. The former refers to discovery of previously unidentified events inside a collection, while the latter strives to identify in real time new events from live news feeds. The experiments show that hierarchical clustering methods are highly informative for retrospective detection of previously unidentified events, while temporal distribution patterns of document clusters provide useful information for improvement in both retrospective detection and online detection of novel events. With the algorithms we propose in Section 4.4 we also target the detection of retrospective events.

Arguing that most of the existing research focusing on retrospective news event detection (RED) make use of only the contents of the news articles, the authors of [LWLM05] propose to do explorations on both content and time information and introduce a probabilistic model to incorporate both content and time information in a unified framework. Similarly, the authors of [FYYL05] also utilize both time and content information. However, in contrast to TDT, which attempts to cluster documents as events using clustering techniques, in [FYYL05] the focus is on detecting a set of bursty features for a bursty event. The main technique employed in the paper is a free probabilistic approach which fully utilizes the time information to determine a set of bursty features which may occur in different time windows. Both [LWLM05, FYYL05] differ from our approach, as we do not take into account any time-related information.

Similar to [FYYL05], in [HCL07] the authors aim to identify feature bursts and their associated bursty periods, by introducing a simple but effective mixture density-based approach. Word trajectories are analyzed in both time and frequency domains, with the specific goal of identifying important and less-reported, periodic and aperiodic events. A set of words with identical trends can be then grouped together to reconstruct an event in a completely unsupervised manner.

A more different approach for detecting events is presented in [CHN08], where the authors propose to use Web click-through data for this purpose. The click-through data is first transformed to a 2D polar space by considering the semantic and temporal dimensions of the queries. Further, robust subspace estimation techniques are applied in order to detect subspaces consisting of only queries with similar semantics and the uninteresting subspaces containing queries not related to real events are pruned. Finally, events are detected from interesting subspaces using a non-parametric clustering technique.

Most of the existing work on event detection focused on identifying events from news corpus collections, and only recently new methods targeting other types of data have been proposed. For example, in [CR09] the authors propose an approach for detecting *Flickr* photos depicting events. Given a set of *Flickr* photos with both user tags and other metadata including time and location (latitude and longitude), the algorithm aims to discover a set of photo groups, where each group corresponds to an event. The method consists of three steps: (1) based on temporal and spatial distributions, tags are identified as related to events or not; (2) after detecting event-related tags, they are further classified into periodic- or aperiodic-event tags; (3) finally, for each tag cluster representing an event, the set of photos corresponding to the event are retrieved. This approach differs from ours in that it relies on geographical information – still inexistent for many pictures. Our method uses solely tag information and has thus a broader applicability.

Another dimension of investigations refers to the work presented in [RGN07]. Focusing also on the domain of pictures, the paper tries to extract event and place semantics from tags assigned to photos in *Flickr*. The proposed approach relies on bursts analysis: tags referring to event names are expected to exhibit high usage patterns over short time periods (maybe also periodical), while location-related tags show these kinds of patterns in the spatial dimension. However like [CR09], [RGN07] also relies on GPS information and has thus a more restricted applicability than our approach.

In [SvZ08], the authors also identify event-related tags by using WordNet. However, event detection is not the main focus of the paper. The focus is rather on a subset of *Flickr* pictures and Sigurbjörnsson and Zwol analyze the different tag categories used by users to annotate their pictures with the aid of WordNet. A tag recommendation algorithm is also proposed in the paper: for a given photo with user-defined tags, the algorithm first derives a list of m candidate tags, based on co-occurrence information. Then, the list is processed and different aggregation and ranking strategies are applied to it, such that a ranked list of n additional tags can be suggested to the user.

The approach presented in [BNG09] is targeting a broader range of data types, namely it tries to identify events and their associated user-contributed social media documents. It thus not only focuses on pictures, but also on music, videos, news and Facebook data. However, the validation of the accuracy of the introduced algorithms is performed on *Flickr* data, having tags corresponding to entries in the Yahoo!'s Upcoming event database[3], and are thus not so extensive like in our case. [BFNP09, BFP09a] are similar to the approach we introduce in Section 4.4, but in this case the focus is on music resources and the authors aim to provide tag recommendations in terms of music themes, moods, genres or styles. Our focus instead is on photo classification and not on tag recommendations.

2.7 Entity Retrieval

Finding entities on the Web is a new IR task which goes beyond the classic document search. While for informational search tasks (see [Bro02] for a classification) document search can give satisfying results for the user, different approaches should be followed when the user is looking for specific entities. For example, when the user wants to find a list of "European female politicians" it is easy for a classical search engine

---

[3]http://www.upcoming.yahoo.com

2.7 Entity Retrieval

to return documents about politics in Europe. It is left to the user to extract the information about the requested entities from the provided results. Our goal is to develop a system that can find entities and not just documents on the Web.

Being able to find entities on the Web can become a new important feature of current search engines. It can allow users to find more than just Web pages, but also people, phone numbers, books, movies, cars, etc. Searching for entities in a collection of documents is not an easy task. Currently, we can see the Web as a set of interlinked pages of different types, e.g. describing tasks, answering questions or describing people. Therefore, in order to find entities, it is necessary to do a preprocessing step of identifying entities in the documents. Moreover, we need to build descriptions of those entities to enable search engines to rank and find them given a user query. Applying classical IR methodologies for finding entities can lead to low effectiveness as seen in previous approaches [BCSW07, CYC07, PVT08]. This is because Entity Retrieval (ER), i.e. finding entities relevant to a query is a task different than document search. Another example of an ER query is "Airports in Germany" where a relevant result is, e.g., "Frankfurt-Hahn Airport". Airports not in Germany or entities other than airports would not be relevant to the given query. It is crucial to rely on consolidated information extraction technologies if we do not want to start with an already high error rate that the ranking algorithms can only increase.

We do not cover work done on the ER task in this thesis; nevertheless, we have addressed it in the following publications: [DFI+10, BID+10, BDF+10, DFG+09, DFI+08, DFIN08, DFI07]. We will continue by providing an overview of ER and its context.

2.7.1 Entity Retrieval Related Tasks

With the current size of the Web and the variety of data it contains, traditional search engines are restricted to simple information needs. Complex queries need, usually, a lot of effort on the user side in order to be satisfied. We can observe different search tasks related to this scenario:

Entity Retrieval. Finding entities of different types is a challenging search task which goes beyond classic document retrieval as well as beyond single-type entity retrieval such as, for example, the popular task of expert finding [BdVCS07]. The motivation for the ER task is that many user queries are not looking for documents to learn about a topic, but really seek a list of specific entities: countries, actors, songs, etc. Examples of such informational needs include "Formula 1 drivers that won the Monaco Grand Prix", "Female singer and songwriter born in Canada", "Swiss cantons where they speak German", and "Coldplay band members". The query "countries where I can pay in Euro" is answered by current web search engines with a list of pages on the topic 'Euro zone', or ways to pay in Euros, but not with a list of country names as the user is asking for. Note that while a single query refers to a single entity type, a system must be able to answer queries for different entity types (differently from an expert search system where the response is always of type person). A commercial prototype performing this task is Google Squared[4].

Question Answering. It must also be mentioned how Entity Retrieval task relates with Question Answering (QA). Common queries in the QA context usually are of type Who, When, Where, Why, How Many. That is, they expect a precise answer as, for example, a number or a name instead of a list of entities. ER queries have considerable similarities with QA "list" questions where the user is looking for a list of items as a result (e.g., "What companies has AARP endorsed?"). In the evaluation benchmarks, QA queries usually consist of sets of questions about a particular topic: this might let the system approach the problem in a different way, e.g., by mining documents retrieved with a keyword query or by exploiting the answer of previous questions on the same topic (e.g., "What does AARP stand for?"). In conclusion, there are similarities between ER and QA queries. In particular for list QA queries we can imagine ER technologies described in this paper exploited, among other things, by QA systems to perform better on this particular type of queries.

Related Entities. Another related task is finding entities similar or related to other entities. In this case the user might have in mind a search query consisting of an example entity. For a given entity, such as "New York", one would expect to find as associated entities places to visit in New York (e.g. "Empire State Building", "Statue of Liberty"), connected historical events (e.g. "September 11, 2001") or famous people (e.g. "Rudy Giuliani"), etc. in a faceted-search fashion. The associated entities can be presented to the user as a lists or grouped by type and other properties (e.g., date). For a query "Albert Einstein", the system may return related entities like, for example, "Germany", "Nobel prize", "physics", "Lieserl Einstein", etc. This task is different from ER as the result set may contain entities of different types. Here the system provides the user with a browsing opportunity rather than with a list of retrieved entities as for ER. A commercial prototype performing this task is Yahoo! Correlator[5].

2.7.2 Application Scenarios for ER

As an initialization step, it is necessary to assign a global identifier for each entity in the collection. Attempts to generate global unique identifiers are already underway, e.g. the OKKAM[6] European Integrated Project is dealing with ID generation on

---

[4]http://www.google.com/squared
[5]http://correlator.sandbox.yahoo.net
[6]http://fp7.okkam.org/

2.7 Entity Retrieval

the Web. One simple application scenario would be ranking consumer products (i.e. entities) where a customer provides as query a list of constraints (e.g. brand, color, size, etc.). ER can be also performed on the Web, where the definition of an entity is not as trivial as in the enterprise example. The entity description will then contain attributes of the entities mentioned in sentences of several Web pages referring to the entity. Relations between entities can then be constructed from links between Web pages as well as references between sentences or paragraphs.

Another application scenario which keeps the main information as in the Web application scenario, but also adds some structure is the Wikipedia model for ER. In this case we consider in D any entity e^i that has its own page in Wikipedia. With this assumption we can easily see these pages as the entity description $d(e^i)$ and the set of the Wikipedia pages that describe an entity as the collection D. Of course, in Wikipedia there are pages which do not describe a particular entity as, for example, the "List of ..." pages. The challenge is to identify which are not entity pages and discard them from D. For each entity the ($<attribute>$, $<value>$) pairs can be build, for example, out of the info-boxes of the Wikipedia pages which contain factual information about the described entity (for example, articles about people contain information about name, birth date, birth place, etc.). In the Wikipedia scenario the sources of information are the people and each s^i_j contributing to $d(e^i)$ can be reconstructed from the edit history of each page allowing also to associate trust values in order to weight more particular sources (see also [AdA07] about such computation). For defining the *type* property in $d(e^i)$ the Wikipedia category information can be used. Relations between entities can be discovered analysing the Wikipedia internal links between pages. The query can be built by the user providing some keywords describing interesting properties plus the selection of a Wikipedia category in order to provide information about the type of entities which are requested. The ranking function $\phi(q, d(e^i))$ should use both information about the properties and the type in order to produce the best ranking.

The specific Wikipedia scenario is slightly different from the general Web scenario as Wikipedia is more clearly structured. It is easy to define an entity as having its own Wikipedia page (i.e. each Wiki page is about one entity) – in the general Web scenario we would have to segment Web pages to extract only sections related to the entity and discard other parts like advertisements or navigational headers. Moreover, it is also easy to extract the entity type from a Wikipedia page, as one of the entity attributes $d(e^i)$, by just considering the Wikipedia categories the page belongs to – the Web scenario would require a thorough Natural Language Processing of the text in order to find phrases describing the entity (e.g. "Mexico *is a* country"). We also make use of the YAGO ontology which is built from Wikipedia and WordNet. If the same system architecture were to be applied to the Web, a new ontology would have to be built in order to make the results comparable. YAGO is also being used in other scenarios than Wikipedia: Revyu.com [HM08] uses Yago class definition in order to assign types to the objects of reviews; in [RSS08] the authors use links between DBpedia and YAGO for interlinking singers, songs, music events, etc. in music datasets. Finally, there is much more content to be found on the Web, while Wikipedia only focuses on some, more common, topics and entities (e.g. we can not find members of a particular organization only from Wikipedia). Nevertheless, Wikipedia is a very good starting point for the emerging task of entity retrieval, and most approaches focus on the Wikipedia scenario. Other algorithms might be developed for ER on the Web still following the proposed model.

2.7.3 Existing ER Approaches

Finding entities on the Web is a recent topic in the IR field. The first proposed approaches [BCSW07, CC07, CYC07] mainly focus on scaling efficiently on Web dimension datasets but not on the effectiveness of search.

A formal model for entities has been presented in [PCAV08]. This entity representation is, similarly to our work, based on ($<attribute>$, $<value>$) pairs and on a "Category of reference" that describes the entity type which can be taken from an ontology. In our work we propose a model for the entire ER process where the entity representation is just a sub-part. A framework for modelling the IR process has been presented in [RTK06] where the authors present a matrix-based framework for modelling possible search tasks.

Approaches for finding entities have also been developed in the Wikipedia context. Previous approaches to rank entities in Wikipedia exploited the link structure between Wikipedia pages [PVT08] or its category structure using graph based algorithms [TSR+08]. Compared to these approaches, we start first designing a model for ER making the development of algorithms possible also in domains different from Wikipedia and we exploit semantic and NLP techniques to improve effectiveness.

Another relevant work is [ZRM+07] which also aims at retrieving entities in Wikipedia but without the assumption that an entity is represented by a Wikipedia page as done in the Initiative for the Evaluation of XML Retrieval (INEX-XER[7]). They rather annotate and retrieve any passage of a Wikipedia article that could represent an entity. A foundation for an effective ER can also be the automatic identification of instances and classes in the Wikipedia category hierarchy [ZNS08]. Knowing which categories describe instances can help the ER system in finding entities relevant to the query because not all the articles in Wikipedia are entity descriptions.

An important related area of research is entity identity on the Web. It is crucial for the ER task being able to uniquely and globally identify entities on the Web so that the search engine can return a list of identifiers to the user who can afterwords navigate in the entity descriptions. A strong discussion already started in the Web research community [BHST08, BSTH07] and solutions for entity identity resolution on the Web have been proposed [BSB08]. Our solution for finding entities relies on

---

[7]http://www.inex.otago.ac.nz/

2.7 Entity Retrieval

these infrastructures able to globally identify entities on the Web.

With respect to our final analysis of easy and difficult topics, a related area is that of query difficulty prediction [CYTS05]. In particular, in [VPN09] they study how to automatically predict the difficulty of an ER query in the Wikipedia context. They also study how to adapt their system variables accordingly in order to improve effectiveness. For example, they use the number of articles attached to categories, the number of categories attached to the entities, query length, etc.

In our work we focus on the Wikipedia corpus and propose algorithms for finding entities based on query relaxation using category information [DFI07]. The main contribution is a methodology for expanding the user query by exploiting the semantic structure of the dataset. Our approach focuses on constructing queries using not only keywords from the query, but also information about relevant categories. This is done leveraging on the highly accurate YAGO ontology [SKW07] which is matched to the character strings of the query. The evaluation is performed using the INEX 2007 Wikipedia collection and entity ranking topics. In [DFIN08] we build on previous algorithms and extend them to use semantics in the context of ER. We adapt the user query by (1) semantic information, (2) Natural Language Processing techniques, and (3) Link Analysis, to rank entities in Wikipedia. We compare different approaches designed for finding entities in Wikipedia and report on results using standard test collections [DFI+10]. An analysis of entity-centric queries reveals different aspects and problems related to ER and shows limitations of current systems performing ER with Wikipedia. It also indicates which approaches are suitable for which kinds of queries.

In [DFI+08] we propose a formal model to define entities as well as a complete ER system, providing examples of its application to enterprise, Web, and Wikipedia scenarios. We present a set of algorithms based on our model and evaluate their retrieval effectiveness. We present an approach for large-scale entity retrieval using Web collections as underlying corpus in [DFG+09]. We propose an architecture for entity extraction and entity ranking starting from Web documents. This is obtained (1) using an existing web documents index and (2) creating an entity centric index. We describe advantages and feasibility of our approach using state-of-the-art tools.

Moving to the Web ER scenario, in [BID+10] we propose a novel approach for ER by using Web search engine query logs. We use Markov random walks on (1) Click Graphs - built from clickt-hrough data - and on (2) Session Graphs - built from user session information. We thus provide semantic bridges between different query terms, and therefore indicate meaningful connections between ER queries and related entities. Experiments are performed on our previously introduced evaluation test set making use of Wikipedia "List of" pages [BDF+10].

3
Search Personalization for the Web

3.1 Introduction

The high importance of Web search engines is no longer a doubt and the booming popularity of search engines has determined simple keyword search to become the only widely accepted user interface for seeking information over the Web. Yet keyword queries are inherently ambiguous. The query "canon book" for example covers several different areas of interest: religion, photography, literature, and music. Clearly, one would prefer search output to be aligned with user's topic(s) of interest, rather than displaying a selection of popular URLs from each category. Studies have shown that more than 80% of the users would prefer to receive such personalized search results [Sul04] instead of the currently generic ones.

In this chapter we tackle the IR area of Search Personalization for textual IR: a user's information need is expressed as a keyword query, on the Web with an average length of 2 to 3 words. Personalization is an effective means to increase Precision of search results. The user will be presented with results ranked both according to his query and to his preferences. One adequate way of accomplishing this purpose is Query Reformulation: modifying the query in such a way that the information need is better reflected. In order to be able to automatically generate reformulations for a given query, we first have to understand the behavior of users who reformulate their queries manually, in several iterations, when no satisfying results are returned by a search engine.

Many Web behavior modeling attempts have been made, building upon simple log statistics [JF03], machine learning [LH99], etc. Yet even though about 50% of the queries are actually reformulation queries [SWJS01], experts still have little understanding of users' search patterns.

Section 3.2 proposes two advances towards modeling the Web search behavior: First, we suggest to use the variation in Query Clarity [CTZC02] as an indicator of user's actions, i.e., generalizing, specializing, or refining the query. Second, we analyze the Part-Of-Speech transitions within reformulation processes and argue that they would make a valuable input for future Web user modeling approaches, in applications such as automatic query expansion, sponsored search, etc. The following section examines the performance of our approaches onto real-life Web search sessions.

Building upon human reformulation behavior, we then present methods to automatically expand a user query with more specific keywords. Query expansion assists the user in formulating a better query, by appending additional keywords to the initial search request in order to encapsulate her interests therein, as well as to focus the Web search output accordingly. It has been shown to perform very well over large data sets, especially with short input queries (see for example [KZ04, CFPS02]). This is exactly the Web search scenario.

Section 3.3 proposes to enhance Web query reformulation by exploiting the user's Personal Information Repository (PIR), i.e., the personal collection of text documents, emails, cached Web pages, etc. Several advantages arise when moving Web search personalization down to the Desktop level (note that by "Desktop" we refer to PIR, and we use the two terms interchangeably). First is of course the quality of personalization: The local Desktop is a rich repository of information, accurately describing most, if not all interests of the user. Second, as all "profile" information is stored and exploited locally, on the personal machine, another very important benefit is privacy. Search engines should not be able to know about a person's interests, i.e., they should not be able to connect a specific person with the queries she issued, or worse, with the output URLs she clicked within the search interface[1] (see Volokh [Vol00] for a discussion on privacy issues related to personalized Web search).

A more direct application of the algorithms presented in Section 3.3 is found in Section 3.4: not only modifying an already existing query, but directly inferring an information need and recommending appropriate solutions to users performing a specific task.

Information is a necessity for many of our tasks, at work or in our personal life, and we simply find no easier way than searching the web for answers to problems. We have to provide means to extract desired information with least effort. In many situations, when a user works on a text file (either reading a web page or a document, or writing an e-mail or a document) he needs other relevant information sources. Characterizing such a file with a few words in order to query a web search engine manually is less intuitive and demands additional effort from the user, so that he would have a strong tendency to sacrifice the results he would have obtained in favor of less work. On the other hand, it would be effortless for the user to just take a look at some recommended web links presented to him or her by a software agent running in the background.

---

[1]Search engines can map queries at least to IP addresses, for example by using cookies and mining the query logs. However, by moving the user profile at the Desktop level we ensure such information is not explicitly associated to a particular user and stored on the search engine side.

Users need additional information related to their work in order to increase the quality of edited content, as well as significantly decrease task working time [RM00]. In order to minimize user effort locating suitable data sources, the PC environment should support the user as much as possible. To accomplish this, we have to understand the tasks the user carries out, then from this user/task-profile extract appropriate information used to query different information sources. Results from a software agent – which tries to understand the user's task and then extracts a list of keywords from a document or a collection of documents – may not be as effective or relevant as results manually retrieved from a search engine – used directly and with a well-known intention by humans. Nevertheless, there are cases where people would not start a web search process by themselves, or not bother to use a search engine in specific stages of their work. Therefore, in Section 3.4, we provide Information Management Assistants (IMA) [BH99] or Just-in-Time IR (JITIR) Agents [RM00] to support the user in this context.

3.2 Query Reformulation Patterns

We start by analyzing human behavior during search. Modeling Web query reformulation processes is still an unsolved problem. In this section we argue that lexical analysis is highly beneficial for this purpose. We propose to use the variation in Query Clarity, as well as the Part-Of-Speech pattern transitions as indicators of users' search actions. Experiments with a log of 2.4 million queries showed our techniques to be more flexible than the current approaches, while also providing us with interesting insights into users' Web behavioral patterns.

Collection

We performed our empirical investigation onto an Excite log of about 2.4 million queries sent over eight hours to the search engine. There were in total 319,566 search sessions, already delimited by the engine in its log using various heuristics (e.g., IP mining, etc.). We further split each session in tasks. Two consecutive queries were assigned to the same task if they contained at least one common non-stopword stem. We thus found 3.08 average tasks per session, and 2.04 average queries per task. Let us now inspect how our two approaches performed.

Defining Reformulation Types

Traditional approaches model reformulation as a function of the number of keywords per search query: (1) Adding terms is related to specializations, removing terms to generalizations, and substituting them to refinements. We argue that this technique is too shallow, and propose to use *Query Clarity* [CTZC02] instead, as an improved indicator of user's actions. We thus build upon the divergence between the language

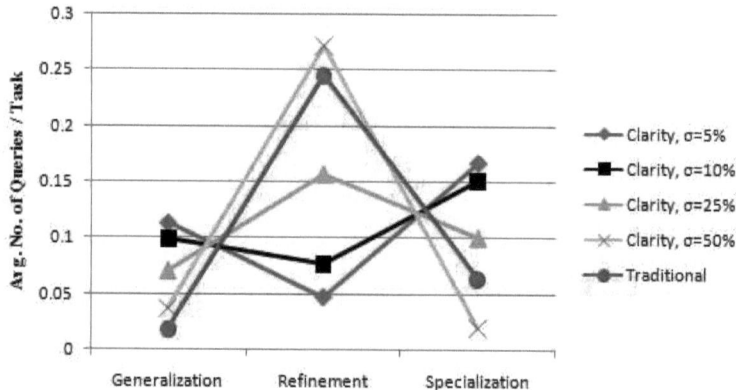

Figure 3.1 Query reformulation patterns as a function of clarity.

From \ To	New Q.	Navigation (by re- sults pages)	Generaliz.	Specializ.	Refinement	Other (Blank Q., Refresh, ...)	Sum From
New Q.	**30.37**	**6.30**	*2.54*	*4.59*	*2.09*	**7.10**	53.00
Navig.	2.27	**16.24**	0.76	*1.40*	0.61	*1.61*	22.91
Gen.	1.61	0.80	0.28	0.92	0.33	0.53	4.51
Spec.	1.83	*1.39*	1.28	0.69	0.55	0.90	6.67
Ref.	1.05	0.70	0.38	0.40	0.46	0.42	3.44
Other	2.09	2.27	0.47	0.78	0.38	*3.42*	9.44
Sum To	39.25	27.73	5.73	8.80	4.45	14.01	100

Table 3.1 Transitions between query types (%).

model associated to the query and that associated to the searched collection. In a simplified version, clarity is expressed as follows:

$$Clarity = \sum_{w \in Query} P_{ml}(w|Query) \cdot log \frac{P_{ml}(w|Query)}{P_{coll}(w)} \quad (3.1)$$

where $P_{ml}(w|Query)$ is the probability of the word w within the query, and $P_{coll}(w)$ is the probability of w within the entire document collection.

In Figure 3.1 we depict the percentage of queries associated to each reformulation pattern, using both the traditional approach and query clarity with different σ values

3.2 Query Reformulation Patterns

From \ To	N.V.Aj.Av	N.V.Aj	N.V.Av	N.Aj.Av	V.Aj.Av	N.V	N.Aj	N.Av	V.Aj	V.Av	Av.Aj	N	V	Aj	Av	U	Sum From
N.V.Aj.Av	*4.45*	0.42	*2.40*	0.67	0.12	0.35	0.14	0.36	0.03	0.06	0.00	0.13	0.03	0.00	0.00	0.02	9.18
N.V.Aj	0.43	0.96	0.31	0.11	0.02	0.95	0.72	0.12	0.13	0.02	0.00	0.65	0.12	0.04	0.00	0.04	4.62
N.V.Av	*2.43*	0.32	*1.47*	0.37	0.07	0.39	0.15	0.27	0.03	0.05	0.00	0.22	0.05	0.01	0.01	0.02	5.85
N.Aj.Av	0.67	0.11	0.37	0.15	0.02	0.09	0.13	0.09	0.01	0.01	0.00	0.09	0.01	0.01	0.00	0.01	1.77
V.Aj.Av	0.12	0.02	0.07	0.02	0.01	0.02	0.01	0.01	0.01	0.00	0.00	0.01	0.00	0.00	0.00	0.00	0.31
N.V	0.36	*1.22*	0.45	0.09	0.02	**6.08**	*1.17*	0.23	0.27	0.04	0.00	*4.72*	0.89	0.06	0.01	0.20	15.81
N.Aj	0.15	0.94	0.17	0.16	0.01	*1.12*	*2.97*	0.30	0.26	0.02	0.01	*2.29*	0.15	0.23	0.01	0.11	8.92
N.Av	0.36	0.14	0.29	0.10	0.01	0.22	0.30	0.29	0.02	0.02	0.00	0.40	0.03	0.02	0.00	0.03	2.26
V.Aj	0.03	0.22	0.04	0.02	0.01	0.29	0.29	0.03	0.16	0.01	0.00	0.23	0.10	0.05	0.00	0.03	1.50
V.Av	0.06	0.02	0.06	0.01	0.00	0.05	0.02	0.03	0.01	0.02	0.01	0.03	0.02	0.00	0.00	0.01	0.35
Av.Aj	0.00	0.00	0.00	0.00	0.01	0.00	0.01	0.01	0.00	0.00	0.01	0.01	0.00	0.01	0.00	0.00	0.07
N (Noun)	0.14	0.90	0.28	0.11	0.01	**6.20**	*3.11*	0.53	0.29	0.04	0.01	**19.45**	*1.14*	0.29	0.02	*1.41*	33.92
V (Verb)	0.03	0.18	0.06	0.01	0.01	*1.48*	0.23	0.04	0.16	0.03	0.00	*1.35*	0.93	0.06	0.01	0.30	4.88
Aj (Adjective)	0.01	0.06	0.01	0.01	0.00	0.11	0.44	0.02	0.09	0.01	0.01	0.33	0.06	0.32	0.01	0.13	1.62
Av (Adverb)	0.00	0.00	0.00	0.00	0.00	0.01	0.02	0.02	0.00	0.01	0.00	0.03	0.01	0.02	0.02	0.01	0.17
U (Unknown)	0.02	0.04	0.02	0.01	0.00	0.32	0.18	0.05	0.04	0.01	0.00	*2.91*	0.61	0.25	0.04	*4.29*	8.78
Sum To	9.26	5.56	6.00	1.85	0.31	17.67	9.91	2.40	1.53	0.35	0.07	32.85	4.14	1.34	0.16	6.61	100

Table 3.2 Part-Of-Speech transitions between various lexical compound patterns (in percentages).

(we take values residing within the $ClarityOfPreviousQuery \pm \sigma$ as denoting refinement queries, values above that interval marking specialization queries, and values below it indicating generalizations). It is obvious to see that introducing "clarity" allows for more flexibility in determining query reformulation actions. The traditional approach is similar to using clarity with a fairly large σ, about 45% of the clarity value of the previous query. Although the best parameter depends on each application, we believe that such a high σ misses out on identifying the *real* underlying intentions of each user, i.e., generalizing or specializing her query. We thus argue that clarity with σ values around 5-10% would model the Web search behavior much better.

We consider a simplified reformulation model as follows: After the first query was issued, if the output is satisfactory, the user would either navigate through the results or start a new search task. Otherwise, she would attempt to improve her query either by narrowing its focus, or by broadening it. Then, the same steps are taken until a satisfactory output is obtained, or until giving up. In Table 3.1 we use clarity with $\sigma = 10\%$ to test our assumptions. Most transitions occur either towards a new query, or towards the next page of results for the current search request (i.e., no reformulation). Unlike with traditional approaches (see Figure 3.1), for clarity the highest amount of reformulations are *specializations*, rather than refinements, which is closer to the intuitive search model outlined above. Also, interestingly, from a specialized query, about 20% of all actions are generalizations, indicating that in some cases users consider to have narrowed their search too much, and thus try to relax it a little bit, again in accordance to the above model.

Part-Of-Speech Pattern Transitions

Applications such as automatic query expansion could be improved by knowing *which* POS are more likely to be added or removed by each user. We thus analyzed the POS transition patterns in Table 3.2. As expected, most queries are composed only of nouns (about 33%). It seems that a good amount of these are ambiguous terms, fact indicated by the high transition rate towards N-V queries (about 20% of all noun queries). We believe this is not due to a real addition of verbs, but rather of multi-sense nouns (e.g., "play", which can act both as a noun and as a verb). Moreover, there are very few queries composed exclusively of adjectives, adverbs, or both, and they usually do not get reformulated at all. The same is valid when a verb is added to the above mentioned patterns. Finally, there is a significant amount of queries containing all 4 major POS, about 10%. The major transition patterns from these queries involve either adding even more words, or removing the adjective(s). Interestingly, queries with N-V-Adv are usually further extended, whereas for queries with N-V-Adj the tendency is to remove words. This indicates that users generally consider N-V-Adv queries to be broad, and thus in need of specialization, whereas N-V-Adj are seen as too specific, or perhaps too badly formulated, which demands for less terms.

Applications

Besides providing an understanding of users' search behavior, reformulation models could be employed in a variety of applications. For example, when the user reformulates her request, the engine could automatically infer that the initial query was not successful, and use this information in order to improve the new search results (e.g., by putting more bias on the newly added terms, for specializations, or by learning which POS transition patterns are characteristic to the user, and consequently adapting automatic query expansion to favor these patterns, etc.).

3.3 Query Expansion Using Desktop Data

Having analyzed user reformulation patterns in the previous section, here we present an approach for automatizing this process. The inherent ambiguity of short keyword queries demands for enhanced methods for Web retrieval. We propose to improve such Web queries by expanding them with terms collected from each user's Personal Information Repository, thus implicitly personalizing the search output. We introduce five broad techniques for generating the additional query keywords by analyzing user data at increasing granularity levels, ranging from term and compound level analysis up to global co-occurrence statistics, as well as to using external thesauri. Our extensive empirical analysis under four different scenarios shows some of these approaches to perform very well, especially on ambiguous queries, producing a very strong increase in the quality of the output rankings. Subsequently, we move this personalized search framework one step further and propose to make the expansion process adaptive to various features of each query. A separate set of experiments indicates the adaptive algorithms to bring an additional statistically significant improvement over the best static expansion approach.

Desktop data represents a very rich repository of profiling information. However, this information comes in a very unstructured way, covering documents which are highly diverse in format, content, and even language characteristics. In this section we first tackle this problem by proposing several lexical analysis algorithms which exploit user's PIR to extract keyword expansion terms at various granularities, ranging from term frequency within Desktop documents up to utilizing global co-occurrence statistics over the personal information repository. Then, in the second part of the section we empirically analyze the performance of each approach.

3.3.1 Algorithms

This section presents the five generic approaches for analyzing user's Desktop data in order to provide expansion terms for Web search. In the proposed algorithms we gradually increase the amount of personal information utilized. Thus, in the first part we investigate three local analysis techniques focused only on those Desktop documents matching user's query best. We append to the Web query the most relevant terms, compounds, and sentence summaries from these documents. In the second part of the section we move towards a global Desktop analysis, proposing to investigate term co-occurrences, as well as thesauri, in the expansion process.

Expanding with Local Desktop Analysis

Local Desktop Analysis is related to enhancing Pseudo Relevance Feedback to generate query expansion keywords from the PIR best hits for user's Web query, rather than from the top ranked Web search results. We distinguish three granularity levels for this process and we investigate each of them separately.

Term and Document Frequency. As the simplest possible measures, TF and DF have the advantage of being very fast to compute. Previous experiments with small data sets have showed them to yield very good results [Eft95]. We thus independently associate a score with each term, based on each of the two statistics. The TF based one is obtained by multiplying the actual frequency of a term with a position score descending as the term first appears closer to the end of the document. This is necessary especially for longer documents, because more informative terms tend to appear towards their beginning [Edm69]. The complete TF based keyword extraction formula is as follows:

$$TermScore = \left[\frac{1}{2} + \frac{1}{2} \cdot \frac{nrWords - pos}{nrWords}\right] \cdot log(1 + TF) \qquad (3.2)$$

where $nrWords$ is the total number of terms in the document and pos is the position of the first appearance of the term; TF represents the frequency of each term in the Desktop document matching user's Web query.

The identification of suitable expansion terms is even simpler when using DF: Given the set of Top-K relevant Desktop documents, generate their snippets as focused on the original search request. This query orientation is necessary, since the DF scores are computed at the level of the entire PIR and would produce too noisy suggestions otherwise. Once the set of candidate terms has been identified, the selection proceeds by ordering them according to the DF scores they are associated with. Ties are resolved using the corresponding TF scores.

Note that a hybrid TFxIDF approach is not necessarily efficient, since one Desktop term might have a high DF on the Desktop, while being quite rare in the Web. For example, the term "PageRank" would be quite frequent on the Desktop of an IR

3.3 Query Expansion Using Desktop Data

scientist, thus achieving a low score with TFxIDF. However, as it is rather rare in the Web, it would make a good resolution of the query towards the correct topic.

Lexical Compounds. Anick and Tipirneni [AT99] defined the *lexical dispersion hypothesis*, according to which an expression's lexical dispersion (i.e., the number of different compounds it appears in within a document or group of documents) can be used to automatically identify key concepts over the input document set. Although several possible compound expressions are available, it has been shown that simple approaches based on noun analysis are almost as good as highly complex part-of-speech pattern identification algorithms [AR02]. We thus inspect the matching Desktop documents for all their lexical compounds of the following form:

$$\{ \; adjective? \; noun+ \; \}$$

All such compounds could be easily generated off-line, at indexing time, for all the documents in the local repository. Moreover, once identified, they can be further sorted depending on their dispersion within each document in order to facilitate fast retrieval of the most frequent compounds at run-time.

Sentence Selection. This technique builds upon sentence oriented document summarization: First, the set of relevant Desktop documents is identified; then, a summary containing their most important sentences is generated as output. Sentence selection is the most comprehensive local analysis approach, as it produces the most detailed expansions (i.e., sentences). Its downside is that, unlike with the first two algorithms, its output cannot be stored efficiently, and consequently it cannot be computed off-line. We generate sentence based summaries by ranking the document sentences according to their salience score, as follows [LAJ01]:

$$SentenceScore = \frac{SW^2}{TW} + PS + \frac{TQ^2}{NQ}$$

The first term is the ratio between the square amount of significant words within the sentence and the total number of words therein. A word is significant in a document if its frequency is above a threshold as follows:

$$TF > ms = \begin{cases} 7 - 0.1 * (25 - NS) & , if \; NS < 25 \\ 7 & , if \; NS \in [25, 40] \\ 7 + 0.1 * (NS - 40) & , if \; NS > 40 \end{cases}$$

with NS being the total number of sentences in the document (see [LAJ01] for details). The second term is a position score set to $(Avg(NS) - SentenceIndex)/Avg^2(NS)$ for the first ten sentences, and to 0 otherwise, $Avg(NS)$ being the average number of sentences over all Desktop items. This way, short documents such as emails are not affected, which is correct, since they usually do not contain a summary in the very beginning. However, as longer documents usually do include overall descriptive sentences in the beginning [Edm69], these sentences are more likely to be relevant.

The final term biases the summary towards the query. It is the ratio between the square number of query terms present in the sentence and the total number of terms from the query. It is based on the belief that the more query terms contained in a sentence, the more likely will that sentence convey information highly related to the query.

Expanding with Global Desktop Analysis

In contrast to the previously presented approach, global analysis relies on information from across the entire personal Desktop to infer the new relevant query terms. In this section we propose two such techniques, namely term co-occurrence statistics, and filtering the output of an external thesaurus.

Term Co-occurrence Statistics. For each term, we can easily compute off-line those terms co-occurring with it most frequently in a given collection (i.e., PIR in our case), and then exploit this information at run-time in order to infer keywords highly correlated with the user query. Our generic co-occurrence based query expansion algorithm is as follows:

Algorithm 3.3.1: Co-occurrence based keyword similarity search.

Off-line computation:
1: Filter potential keywords k with $DF \in [10, \ldots, 20\% \cdot N]$
2: For each keyword k_i
3:   **For** each keyword k_j
4:   Compute SC_{k_i,k_j}, the similarity coefficient of (k_i, k_j)

On-line computation:
1: Let S be the set of keywords,
         potentially similar to an input expression E.
2: For each keyword k of E:
3: $S \leftarrow S \cup TSC(k)$, where $TSC(k)$ contains the
                    Top-K terms most similar to k
4: For each term t of S:
5a: **Let** $Score(t) \leftarrow \prod_{k \in E}(0.01 + SC_{t,k})$
5b: **Let** $Score(t) \leftarrow \#DesktopHits(E|t)$
6: Select Top-K terms of S with the highest scores.

The off-line computation needs an initial trimming phase (step 1) for optimization purposes. In addition, we also restricted the algorithm to computing co-occurrence levels across nouns only, as they contain by far the largest amount of conceptual

3.3 Query Expansion Using Desktop Data

information, and as this approach reduces the size of the co-occurrence matrix considerably. During the run-time phase, having the terms most correlated with each particular query keyword already identified, one more operation is necessary, namely calculating the correlation of every output term with the entire query. Two approaches are possible: (1) using a product of the correlation between the term and all keywords in the original expression (step 5a), or (2) simply counting the number of documents in which the proposed term co-occurs with the entire user query (step 5b). We considered the following formulas for Similarity Coefficients [KC99]:

- *Cosine Similarity*, defined as:

$$CS = \frac{DF_{x,y}}{\sqrt{DF_x \cdot DF_y}} \quad (3.3)$$

- *Mutual Information*, defined as:

$$MI = \log \frac{N \cdot DF_{x,y}}{DF_x \cdot DF_y} \quad (3.4)$$

- *Likelihood Ratio*, defined in the paragraphs below.

DF_x is the Document Frequency of term x, and $DF_{x,y}$ is the number of documents containing both x and y. To further increase the quality of the generated scores we limited the latter indicator to co-occurrences within a window of W terms. We set W to be the same as the maximum amount of expansion keywords desired.

Dunning's Likelihood Ratio λ [Dun93] is a co-occurrence based metric similar to χ^2. It starts by attempting to reject the null hypothesis, according to which two terms A and B would appear in text independently from each other. This means that $P(A\ B) = P(A\ \neg B) = P(A)$, where $P(A\ \neg B)$ is the probability that term A is *not* followed by term B. Consequently, the test for independence of A and B can be performed by looking if the distribution of A given that B is present is the same as the distribution of A given that B is not present. Of course, in reality we know these terms are not independent in text, and we only use the statistical metrics to highlight terms which are frequently appearing together. We compare the two binomial processes by using likelihood ratios of their associated hypotheses. First, let us define the likelihood ratio for one hypothesis:

$$\lambda = \frac{max_{\omega \in \Omega_0} H(\omega; k)}{max_{\omega \in \Omega} H(\omega; k)} \quad (3.5)$$

where ω is a point in the parameter space Ω, Ω_0 is the particular hypothesis being tested, and k is a point in the space of observations K. If we assume that two binomial distributions have the same underlying parameter, i.e., $\{(p_1, p_2) \mid p_1 = p_2\}$, we can write:

$$\lambda = \frac{max_p H(p, p; k_1, k_2, n_1, n_2)}{max_{p_1, p_2} H(p_1, p_2; k_1, k_2, n_1, n_2)} \quad (3.6)$$

where $H(p_1, p_2; k_1, k_2, n_1, n_2) = p_1^{k_1} \cdot (1 - p_1)^{(n_1 - k_1)} \cdot \binom{n_1}{k_1} \cdot p_2^{k_2} \cdot (1 - p_2)^{(n_2 - k_2)} \cdot \binom{n_2}{k_2}$. Since the maxima are obtained with $p_1 = \frac{k_1}{n_1}$, $p_2 = \frac{k_2}{n_2}$, and $p = \frac{k_1 + k_2}{n_1 + n_2}$, we have:

$$\lambda = \frac{max_p L(p, k_1, n_1) L(p, k_2, n_2)}{max_{p_1, p_2} L(p_1, k_1, n_1) L(p_2, k_2, n_2)} \quad (3.7)$$

where $L(p, k, n) = p^k \cdot (1-p)^{n-k}$. Taking the logarithm of the likelihood, we obtain:

$$-2 \cdot log\ \lambda = \quad 2 \cdot [log\ L(p_1, k_1, n_1) + log\ L(p_2, k_2, n_2) - \\ log\ L(p, k_1, n_1) - log\ L(p, k_2, n_2)]$$

where $log\ L(p, k, n) = k \cdot log\ p + (n-k) \cdot log(1-p)$. Finally, if we write $O_{11} = P(A\ B)$, $O_{12} = P(\neg A\ B)$, $O_{21} = P(A\ \neg B)$, and $O_{22} = P(\neg A\ \neg B)$, then the co-occurrence likelihood of terms A and B becomes:

$$-2 \cdot log\ \lambda = \quad 2 \cdot [O_{11} \cdot log\ p_1 + O_{12} \cdot log\ (1-p_1) + \\ O_{21} \cdot log\ p_2 + O_{22} \cdot log\ (1-p_2) - \\ (O_{11} + O_{21}) \cdot log\ p - (O_{12} + O_{22}) \cdot log\ (1-p)]$$

where $p_1 = \frac{k_1}{n_1} = \frac{O_{11}}{O_{11}+O_{12}}$, $p_2 = \frac{k_2}{n_2} = \frac{O_{21}}{O_{21}+O_{22}}$, and $p = \frac{k_1+k_2}{n_1+n_2}$.

Thesaurus Based Expansion. Large scale thesauri encapsulate global knowledge about term relationships. Thus, we first identify the set of terms closely related to each query keyword, and then we calculate the Desktop co-occurrence level of each of these possible expansion terms with the entire initial search request. In the end, those suggestions with the highest frequencies are kept. The algorithm is as follows:

Algorithm 3.3.2: Filtered thesaurus based query expansion.

1: **For** each keyword k of an input query Q:
2:     **Select** the following sets of related terms using WordNet:
2a: Syn: All Synonyms
2b: Sub: All sub-concepts residing one level below k
2c: Super: All super-concepts residing one level above k
3: **For** each set S_i of the above mentioned sets:
4:     **For** each term t of S_i:
5:         **Search** the PIR with $(Q|t)$, i.e.,
            the original query, as expanded with t
6:         **Let** H be the number of hits of the above search
            (i.e., the co-occurence level of t with Q)
7:     **Return** Top-K terms as ordered by their H values.

We observe three types of term relationships (steps 2a-2c): (1) synonyms, (2) sub-concepts, namely hyponyms (i.e., sub-classes) and meronyms (i.e., sub-parts), and (3) super-concepts, namely hypernyms (i.e., super-classes) and holonyms (i.e., super-parts). As they represent quite different types of association, we investigated them separately. We limited the output expansion set (step 7) to contain only terms appearing at least T times on the Desktop, in order to avoid noisy suggestions, with $T = min(\frac{N}{DocsPerTopic}, MinDocs)$. We set $DocsPerTopic = 2,500$, and $MinDocs = 5$, the latter one coping with the case of small PIRs.

3.3 Query Expansion Using Desktop Data   47

Evaluation

Experimental Setup

We evaluated our algorithms with 18 subjects (Ph.D. and Post-Doc. students in different areas of computer science and education). First, they installed our Lucene based search engine[2] and indexed all their locally stored content: Files within user selected paths, Emails, and Web Cache. Without loss of generality, we focused the experiments on single-user machines. Then, they chose 4 queries related to their everyday activities, as follows:

- One very frequent AltaVista query, as extracted from the top 2% queries most issued to the search engine within a 7.2 million entries log from October 2001. In order to connect such a query to each user's interests, we added an off-line pre-processing phase: We generated the most frequent search requests and then randomly selected a query with at least 10 hits on each subject's Desktop. To further ensure a real life scenario, users were allowed to reject the proposed query and ask for a new one, if they considered it totally outside their interest areas.
- One randomly selected log query, filtered using the same procedure as above.
- One self-selected specific query, which they thought to have only one meaning.
- One self-selected ambiguous query, which they thought to have at least three meanings.

The average query lengths were 2.0 and 2.3 terms for the log queries, as well as 2.9 and 1.8 for the self-selected ones. Even though our algorithms are mainly intended to enhance search when using ambiguous query keywords, we chose to investigate their performance on a wide span of query types, in order to see how they perform in all situations. The log queries evaluate real life requests, in contrast to the self-selected ones, which target rather the identification of top and bottom performances. Note that the former ones were somewhat farther away from each subject's interest, thus being also more difficult to personalize on. To gain an insight into the relationship between each query type and user interests, we asked each person to rate the query itself with a score of 1 to 5, having the following interpretations: (1) never heard of it, (2) do not know it, but heard of it, (3) know it partially, (4) know it well, (5) major interest. The obtained grades were 3.11 for the top log queries, 3.72 for the randomly selected ones, 4.45 for the self-selected specific ones, and 4.39 for the self-selected ambiguous ones.

For each query, we collected the Top-5 URLs generated by 20 versions of the algorithms[3] presented in Section 3.3.1. These results were then shuffled into one set

---

[2] Clearly, if one had already installed a Desktop search application, then this overhead would not be present.

[3] Note that all Desktop level parts of our algorithms were performed with Lucene using its predefined searching and ranking functions.

containing usually between 70 and 90 URLs. Thus, each subject had to assess about 325 documents for all four queries, being neither aware of the algorithm, nor of the ranking of each assessed URL. Overall, 72 queries were issued and over 6,000 URLs were evaluated during the experiment. For each of these URLs, the testers had to give a rating ranging from 0 to 2, dividing the relevant results in two categories, (1) relevant and (2) highly relevant. Finally, the quality of each ranking was assessed using the normalized version of Discounted Cumulative Gain (DCG) [JK00]. DCG is a rich measure, as it gives more weight to highly ranked documents, while also incorporating different relevance levels by giving them different gain values:

$$DCG(i) = \begin{cases} G(1) & , if\ i = 1 \\ DCG(i-1) + G(i)/log(i) & , otherwise. \end{cases}$$

We used G(i) = 1 for relevant results, and G(i) = 2 for highly relevant ones. As queries having more relevant output documents will have a higher DCG, we also normalized its value to a score between 0 (the worst possible DCG given the ratings) and 1 (the best possible DCG given the ratings) to facilitate averaging over queries. All results were tested for statistical significance using T-tests.

Algorithmic specific aspects. The main parameter of our algorithms is the number of generated expansion keywords. For this experiment we set it to 4 terms for all techniques, leaving an analysis at this level for a subsequent investigation. In order to optimize the run-time computation speed, we chose to limit the number of output keywords per Desktop document to the number of expansion keywords desired (i.e., four). For all algorithms we also investigated bigger limitations. This allowed us to observe that the Lexical Compounds method would perform better if only at most one compound per document were selected. We therefore chose to experiment with this new approach as well. For all other techniques, considering less than four terms per document did not seem to consistently yield any additional qualitative gain. We labeled the algorithms we evaluated as follows:

0. **Google**: The actual Google query output, as returned by the Google API;
1. **TF, DF**: Term and Document Frequency;
2. **LC, LC[O]**: Regular and Optimized (by considering only one top compound per document) Lexical Compounds;
3. **SS**: Sentence Selection;
4. **TC[CS], TC[MI], TC[LR]**: Term Co-occurrence Statistics using respectively Cosine Similarity, Mutual Information, and Likelihood Ratio as similarity coefficients;
5. **WN[SYN], WN[SUB], WN[SUP]**: WordNet based expansion with synonyms, sub-concepts, and super-concepts, respectively.

Except for the thesaurus based expansion, in all cases we also investigated the performance of our algorithms when exploiting only the Web browser cache to represent user's personal information. This is motivated by the fact that other personal documents such as for example emails are known to have a somewhat different language

3.3 Query Expansion Using Desktop Data

than that residing on the world wide Web [TDH05]. However, as this approach performed visibly poorer than using the entire Desktop data, we omitted it from the subsequent analysis.

Results

Log Queries. We evaluated all variants of our algorithms using NDCG. For log queries, the best performance was achieved with TF, LC[O], and TC[LR]. The improvements they brought were up to 5.2% for top queries ($p = 0.14$) and 13.8% for randomly selected queries ($p = 0.01$, statistically significant), both obtained with LC[O]. A summary of all results is depicted in Table 3.3.

Both TF and LC[O] yielded very good results, indicating that simple keyword and expression oriented approaches might be sufficient for the Desktop based query expansion task. LC[O] was much better than LC, ameliorating its quality with up to 25.8% in the case of randomly selected log queries, improvement which was also significant with $p = 0.04$. Thus, a selection of compounds spanning over several Desktop documents is more informative about user's interests than the general approach, in which there is no restriction on the number of compounds produced from every personal item.

The more complex Desktop oriented approaches, namely sentence selection and all term co-occurrence based algorithms, showed a rather average performance, with no visible improvements, except for TC[LR]. Also, the thesaurus based expansion usually produced very few suggestions, possibly because of the many technical queries employed by our subjects. We observed however that expanding with sub-concepts is very good for everyday life terms (e.g., "car"), whereas the use of super-concepts is valuable for compounds having at least one term with low technicality (e.g., "document clustering"). As expected, the synonym based expansion performed generally well, though in some very technical cases it yielded rather general suggestions. Finally, we noticed Google to be very optimized for some top frequent queries. However, even within this harder scenario, some of our personalization algorithms produced statistically significant improvements over regular search (i.e., TF and LC[O]).

Self-selected Queries. The NDCG values obtained with self-selected queries are depicted in Table 3.4. While our algorithms did not enhance Google for the clear search tasks, they did produce strong improvements of up to 52.9% (which were of course also highly significant with $p \ll 0.01$) when utilized with ambiguous queries. In fact, almost all our algorithms resulted in statistically significant improvements over Google for this query type.

In general, the relative differences between our algorithms were similar to those observed for the log based queries. As in the previous analysis, the simple Desktop based Term Frequency and Lexical Compounds metrics performed best. Nevertheless, a very good outcome was also obtained for Desktop based sentence selection and all term co-occurrence metrics. There were no visible differences between the behavior

Algorithm	NDCG Top	Signific. vs. Google	NDCG Random	Signific. vs. Google
Google	0.42	-	0.40	-
TF	**0.43**	**p = 0.32**	**0.43**	**p = 0.04**
DF	0.17	-	0.23	-
LC	0.39	-	0.36	-
LC[O]	**0.44**	**p = 0.14**	**0.45**	**p = 0.01**
SS	0.33	-	0.36	-
TC[CS]	0.37	-	0.35	-
TC[MI]	0.40	-	0.36	-
TC[LR]	**0.41**	-	**0.42**	**p = 0.06**
WN[SYN]	0.42	-	0.38	-
WN[SUB]	0.28	-	0.33	-
WN[SUP]	0.26	-	0.26	-

Table 3.3 Normalized Discounted Cumulative Gain at the first 5 results when searching for top (left) and random (right) log queries.

Algorithm	NDCG Clear	Signific. vs. Google	NDCG Ambiguous	Signific. vs. Google
Google	0.71	-	0.39	-
TF	**0.66**	-	**0.52**	**p ≪ 0.01**
DF	0.37	-	0.31	-
LC	**0.65**	-	**0.54**	**p ≪ 0.01**
LC[O]	**0.69**	-	**0.59**	**p ≪ 0.01**
SS	**0.56**	-	**0.52**	**p ≪ 0.01**
TC[CS]	**0.60**	-	**0.50**	**p = 0.01**
TC[MI]	**0.60**	-	**0.47**	**p = 0.02**
TC[LR]	**0.56**	-	**0.47**	**p = 0.03**
WN[SYN]	0.70	-	0.36	-
WN[SUB]	0.46	-	0.32	-
WN[SUP]	0.51	-	0.29	-

Table 3.4 Normalized Discounted Cumulative Gain at the first 5 results when searching for user selected clear (left) and ambiguous (right) queries.

of the three different approaches to co-occurrence calculation. Finally, for the case of clear queries, we noticed that fewer expansion terms than 4 might be less noisy and thus helpful in bringing further improvements. We thus pursued this idea with the adaptive algorithms presented in the next section.

3.3 Query Expansion Using Desktop Data 51

3.3.2 Introducing Adaptivity

In the previous section we have investigated the behavior of each technique when adding a fixed number of keywords to the user query. However, an optimal personalized query expansion algorithm should automatically adapt itself to various aspects of each query, as well as to the particularities of the person using it. In this section we discuss the factors influencing the behavior of our expansion algorithms, which might be used as input for the adaptivity process. Then, in the second part we present some initial experiments with one of them, namely query clarity.

Adaptivity Factors

Several indicators could assist the algorithm to automatically tune the number of expansion terms. We start by discussing adaptation by analyzing the query clarity level. Then, we briefly introduce an approach to model the generic query formulation process in order to tailor the search algorithm automatically, and discuss some other possible factors that might be of use for this task.

Query Clarity. The interest for analyzing query difficulty has increased only recently, and there are not many papers addressing this topic. Yet it has been long known that query disambiguation has a high potential of improving retrieval effectiveness for low recall searches with very short queries [KC92], which is exactly our targeted scenario. Also, the success of IR systems clearly varies across different topics. We thus propose to use an estimate number expressing the calculated level of query clarity in order to automatically tweak the amount of personalization fed into the algorithm. The following metrics are available:

- *The Query Length* is expressed simply by the number of words in the user query. The solution is rather inefficient, as reported by He and Ounis [HO04].
- *The Query Scope* relates to the IDF of the entire query, as in:

$$C_1 = log(\frac{\#DocumentsInCollection}{\#Hits(Query)}) \tag{3.8}$$

This metric performs well when used with document collections covering a single topic, but poor otherwise [CTZC02, HO04].

- *The Query Clarity* [CTZC02] seems to be the best, as well as the most applied technique so far. It measures the divergence between the language model associated to the user query and the language model associated to the collection. In a simplified version (i.e., without smoothing over the terms which are not present in the query), it can be expressed as follows:

$$C_2 = \sum_{w \in Query} P_{ml}(w|Query) \cdot log\frac{P_{ml}(w|Query)}{P_{coll}(w)} \tag{3.9}$$

where $P_{ml}(w|Query)$ is the probability of the word w within the submitted query, and $P_{coll}(w)$ is the probability of w within the entire collection of documents.

Other solutions exist, but we think they are too computationally expensive for the huge amount of data that needs to be processed within Web applications. We thus decided to investigate only C_1 and C_2. First, we analyzed their performance over a large set of queries and split their clarity predictions in three categories:

- Small Scope / Clear Query: $C_1 \in [0, 12], C_2 \in [4, \infty)$.
- Medium Scope / Semi-Ambiguous Query:
  $C_1 \in [12, 17), C_2 \in [2.5, 4)$.
- Large Scope / Ambiguous Query:
  $C_1 \in [17, \infty), C_2 \in [0, 2.5]$.

In order to limit the amount of experiments, we analyzed only the results produced when employing C_1 for the PIR and C_2 for the Web. As algorithmic basis we used LC[O], i.e., optimized lexical compounds, which was clearly the winning method in the previous analysis. As manual investigation showed it to slightly overfit the expansion terms for clear queries, we utilized a substitute for this particular case. Two candidates were considered: (1) TF, i.e., the second best approach, and (2) WN[SYN], as we observed that its first and second expansion terms were often very good.

Given the algorithms and clarity measures, we implemented the adaptivity procedure by tailoring the amount of expansion terms added to the original query, as a function of its ambiguity in the Web, as well as within user's PIR. Note that the ambiguity level is related to the number of documents covering a certain query. Thus, to some extent, it has different meanings on the Web and within PIRs. While a query deemed ambiguous on a large collection such as the Web will very likely indeed have a large number of meanings, this may not be the case for the Desktop. Take for example the query "PageRank". If the user is a link analysis expert, many of her documents might match this term, and thus the query would be classified as ambiguous. However, when analyzed against the Web, this is definitely a clear query. Consequently, we employed more additional terms, when the query was more ambiguous in the Web, but also on the Desktop. Put another way, queries deemed clear on the Desktop were inherently not well covered within user's PIR, and thus had fewer keywords appended to them. The number of expansion terms we utilized for each combination of scope and clarity levels is depicted in Table 3.5.

Query Formulation Process. Interactive query expansion has a high potential for enhancing search [Rut03]. We believe that modeling its underlying process would be very helpful in producing qualitative adaptive Web search algorithms. For example, when the user is adding a new term to her previously issued query, she is basically reformulating her original request. Thus, the newly added terms are more likely to convey information about her search goals. For a general, non personalized retrieval

3.3 Query Expansion Using Desktop Data

Desktop Scope	Web Clarity	No. of Terms	Algorithm
Large	Ambiguous	4	LC[O]
Large	Semi-Ambig.	3	LC[O]
Large	Clear	2	LC[O]
Medium	Ambiguous	3	LC[O]
Medium	Semi-Ambig.	2	LC[O]
Medium	Clear	1	TF / WN[SYN]
Small	Ambiguous	2	TF / WN[SYN]
Small	Semi-Ambig.	1	TF / WN[SYN]
Small	Clear	0	-

Table 3.5 Adaptive Personalized Query Expansion.

engine, this could correspond to giving more weight to these new keywords. Within our personalized scenario, the generated expansions can similarly be biased towards these terms. Nevertheless, more investigations are necessary in order to solve the challenges posed by this approach.

Other Features. The idea of adapting the retrieval process to various aspects of the query, of the user itself, and even of the employed algorithm has received only little attention in the literature. Only some approaches have been investigated, usually indirectly. There exist studies of query behaviors at different times of day, or of the topics spanned by the queries of various classes of users, etc. However, they generally do not discuss how these features can be actually incorporated in the search process itself and they have almost never been related to the task of Web personalization.

Evaluation

We used exactly the same experimental setup as for our previous analysis, with two log-based queries and two self-selected ones (all different from before, in order to make sure there is no bias on the new approaches), evaluated with NDCG over the Top-5 results output by each algorithm. The newly proposed adaptive personalized query expansion algorithms are denoted as A[LCO/TF] for the approach using TF with the clear Desktop queries, and as A[LCO/WN] when WN[SYN] was utilized instead of TF.

The overall results were at least similar, or better than Google for all kinds of log queries (see Table 3.6). For top frequent queries, both adaptive algorithms, A[LCO/TF] and A[LCO/WN], improve with 10.8% and 7.9% respectively, both differences being also statistically significant with $p \leq 0.01$. They also achieve an improvement of up to 6.62% over the best performing static algorithm, LC[O] ($p = 0.07$). For randomly selected queries, even though A[LCO/TF] yields significantly better results than Google ($p = 0.04$), both adaptive approaches fall behind the static algorithms.

Algorithm	NDCG Top	Signific. vs. Google	NDCG Random	Signific. vs. Google
Google	0.51	-	0.45	-
TF	0.51	-	0.48	p = 0.04
LC[O]	0.53	p = 0.09	0.52	p < 0.01
WN[SYN]	0.51	-	0.45	-
A[LCO/TF]	0.56	p < 0.01	0.49	p = 0.04
A[LCO/WN]	0.55	p = 0.01	0.44	-

Table 3.6 Normalized Discounted Cumulative Gain at the first 5 results when using our *adaptive* personalized search algorithms on top (left) and random (right) log queries.

Algorithm	NDCG Clear	Signific. vs. Google	NDCG Ambiguous	Signific. vs. Google
Google	0.81	-	0.46	-
TF	0.76	-	0.54	p = 0.03
LC[O]	0.77	-	0.59	p ≪ 0.01
WN[SYN]	0.79	-	0.44	-
A[LCO/TF]	0.81	-	0.64	p ≪ 0.01
A[LCO/WN]	0.81	-	0.63	p ≪ 0.01

Table 3.7 Normalized Discounted Cumulative Gain at the first 5 results when using our *adaptive* personalized search algorithms on user selected clear (left) and ambiguous (right) queries.

The major reason seems to be the imperfect selection of the number of expansion terms, as a function of query clarity. Thus, more experiments are needed in order to determine the optimal number of generated expansion keywords, as a function of the query ambiguity level.

The analysis of the self-selected queries shows that adaptivity can bring even further improvements into Web search personalization (see Table 3.7). For ambiguous queries, the scores given to Google search are enhanced by 40.6% through A[LCO/TF] and by 35.2% through A[LCO/WN], both strongly significant with $p \ll 0.01$. Adaptivity also brings another 8.9% improvement over the static personalization of LC[O] ($p = 0.05$). Even for clear queries, the newly proposed flexible algorithms perform slightly better, improving with 0.4% and 1.0% respectively.

All results are depicted graphically in Figure 3.2. We notice that A[LCO/TF] is the overall best algorithm, performing better than Google for all types of queries, either extracted from the search engine log, or self-selected. The experiments presented in this section confirm clearly that adaptivity is a necessary further step to take in Web search personalization.

3.4 Recommending Related Web Pages to User Tasks

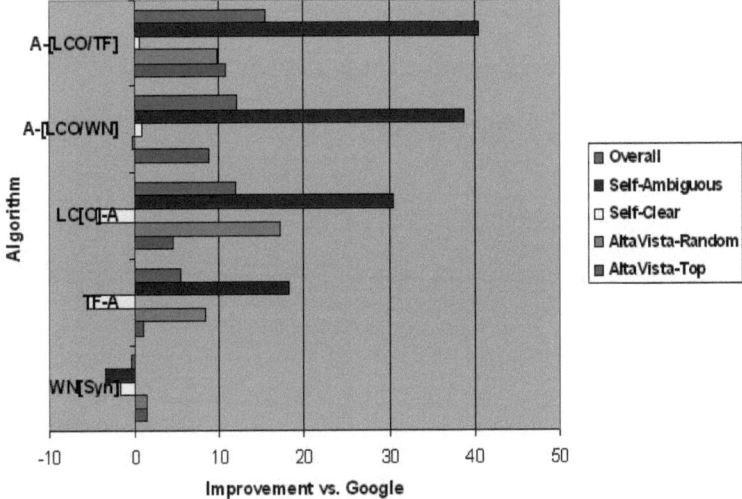

Figure 3.2 Relative NDCG gain (in %) for each algorithm overall, as well as separated per query category.

3.4 Recommending Related Web Pages to User Tasks

Searching the web has become a task in many people's work, without which subsequent tasks would be hard to carry out or even impossible. But as people tend to have less time for querying the web or even for searching their personal computer for information they need, it becomes common to skip information gathering activities like trying to find useful resources on the web because of the "effort" it takes to query a web search engine. Starting from the previously presented algorithms, we modify them and apply them in the case of an unexpressed, latent user information need extracted from the currently performed user task. In this section we propose to use software agents that collect useful web specific related information which would otherwise not be viewed at all. More specifically, we present methods to automatically search the web and recommend URLs relevant to user's current work, defined through his or her active personal desktop documents. Our experiments show our proposed algorithms, Sentence Selection and Lexical Compounds, to yield significant improvement over simple Term Frequency based web query generation, which we used as a baseline.

3.4.1 Extracting Relevant Query Keywords

We will consider one current document – an email, a web page or another document containing text – as an input file. From this input file the software agent has to deduct the task the user is currently working on. The current task will be represented as series of keywords. These keywords have to cover the topics present in the analyzed document, and represent each topic accurately. To accomplish these tasks we use three algorithms presented in Section 3.3.1: Term Frequency, Sentence Selection and Lexical Compounds. The number of extracted keywords is limited to 20 or the number of sentences the input file contains multiplied by two, whichever number is smaller, to ensure that only relevant keywords are extracted. If we use a larger number of keywords, then the probability that some of these keywords do not represent the current user task grows exponentially.

Term Frequency. As presented in Section 3.3.1, the Term Frequency (TF) algorithm will be used throughout this section as a baseline to compare our other two algorithms with.

Sentence Selection. We adapted the Sentence Selection (SS) algorithm to suite our particular setting. From the input document we extracted the most salient sentences with respect to the user query by evaluating the following formula in the case of keyword extraction from the current document:

$$SentenceScore_{single} = \frac{SW^2}{TW}$$

When performing Sentence Selection over similar desktop documents we use the following extended formula:

$$SentenceScore_{desktop} = \frac{SW^2}{TW} + \frac{NQ^2}{TQ}$$

With the first term being the ratio between the square amount of significant words within the sentence and the total number of words therein, and the second term being computed using the ratio between the square number of query terms present in the sentence (NQ) and the total number of terms (TQ) from the query. Note that in our case the query is formed of keywords extracted from the initial input file.

Once these sentence scores were computed, we sought for query expansion terms combining two approaches: (1) extracting the terms with the highest term frequency in the documents the sentences originate from, over the top 9 sentences, as reported in [LAJ01], and (2) using the same approach but over the top 2% sentences. The new latter approach is motivated by previous findings that longer documents tend to contain more topics, ant thus more content words [Kat96] and does indeed slightly improve over the former one. We combined these two approaches as to use 2% sentences per document but still a minimum of 9 sentences.

3.4 Recommending Related Web Pages to User Tasks   **57**

Lexical Compounds. We used the Lexical Compounds (*LC*) approach as presented above in Section 3.3.1. Once the lexical constructions have been identified, they are sorted depending on their dispersion within the document, and the terms of the most frequent ten compounds (as most of the compounds consist of two words) are used as query expansion keywords.

3.4.2 Recommending Related Web Pages

We now need to efficiently use these keywords in order to locate web pages relevant to user's current task. After extracting task descriptive keywords from the active document, one of two methods can be applied for each of the described algorithms.

Exploiting only the Currently Active Document

The first method we used is regarding the currently active document as sufficient task context, as to create a complete current user task image. Since the output from the algorithms is a sorted by importance list of terms, the selected keywords can be used directly to form a query, which is then used in conjunction with Google API[4] to retrieve the relevant URLs to be presented to the user. The only restriction applied is limiting the number of keywords used to form the query to a maximum of 20 terms or twice the number of sentences in the analyzed document. Thus, the web search query is formed by just concatenating the list of sorted space delimited keywords, since the Google API does not allow us to specify different weights for each query term.

Exploiting the Full Context of the Currently Active Document

There are cases when the currently active document does not provide sufficient information for the software agent to fully understand the user task. Therefore we need to supply additional information by using also other context related documents from the user's PC. For the software agent this translates into retrieving similar documents from the desktop by using the previously computed keywords (i.e., the output from each algorithm). The document retrieval is being achieved using the Lucene search engine. The number of keywords for finding similar desktop documents may be diminished until at least two documents are retrieved that contain all the searched keywords. For time saving reasons and due to the just-in-time nature of the software agent, only the top 10 desktop documents from the hits list are considered. The same keyword extraction algorithm is then applied to these retrieved desktop documents and another list of keywords is extracted. The two keyword lists, the one resulting from the initial document and the one extracted from the related desktop documents, are then combined in such a way that the number of keywords from each source is equal, but the weight of the keywords extracted from the initial document

---

[4]http://api.google.com

the user is working on is higher. When used with Google API, this translates into creating a web search query consisting of the first (maximum) 10 keywords from the initial document, followed by keywords from the desktop, to the maximum sum of 20 keywords.

The final query issued to Google API consisted only of English words listed in WordNet [Mil95] as we noticed that without this restraint, some very user specific terms that are not found within documents on the internet could also be included. We also excluded keywords consisting of less than three characters, as they are usually abbreviations, and the abbreviations coming from the user desktop can be in many cases created by that user and have different meanings even throughout the same interest community.

3.4.3 Evaluation

Experimental Setup

Prior to running the main software agent, the entire desktop content i.e., all the files on the user's computer have to be indexed for future faster retrieval. The Lucene[5] information retrieval system suits our interests best, given its rapid search algorithms, its flexibility and adaptivity and last but not least its cross-platform portability. We have used Lucene to index the user's desktop contents for subsequent faster access to those files. We defined "PC Desktop" as the collection of all emails, web cache documents, and indexable files of a user. For the latter ones, we did not index the entire hard disks, but only the list of paths containing personal documents, as specified by each person[6].

Following the work of Lam et al. [LAJ01], we chose to index only documents with at least 7 indexable terms (i.e., not stopwords). Moreover, we defined several heuristics to exclude from the index some very common automatically generated file categories such as Java documentation, as their large granularity tended to negatively influence the desktop summaries. Finally, in all cases but one, we only used TF, rather than $TFxIDF$, as one very frequent local term (e.g., PageRank) might in fact be rather rare in the web. A large stopword list was used to initially remove any possible misleading terms. Also, summarization was achieved employing $logTF$ rather than TF in order to avoid having some too frequent terms mislead the results. The variants of TF and IDF we used were as follows:

$$TF_{t_k,D_j} = \begin{cases} 0 & \text{, if } TF'_{t_k,D_j} = 0 \\ 1 + log(TF'_{t_k,D_j}) & \text{, otherwise} \end{cases}$$
$$IDF_{t_k} = log(1 + \frac{N}{DF_{t_k}})$$

---

[5]http://lucene.apache.org
[6]Although this definition was targeted at single-user PCs, one could easily extend it to multiple-user ones.

3.4 Recommending Related Web Pages to User Tasks

Input type	min	med	max
Email	5	15	all
Document	10	25	all
Web page	-	-	all

Table 3.8 Number of sentences used for the simulation of a work in progress

where TF'_{t_k,D_j} is the actual frequency of term t_k in document D_j, N is the total number of documents in the collection and DF_{t_k} is the document frequency for term t_k.

We started our analysis by manually inspecting the output of each keyword extraction algorithm. In most cases, we found it to be quite representative for the original document or set of documents, i.e. extracting the main topic keywords from the given text. However, as in other similar works (e.g., [LAJ01]), our main objective measure of quality was its overall precision in recommending related web page, and thus we will focus our presentation only towards this aspect.

To evaluate the precision of our personalization algorithms we interviewed 13 researchers in different computer science areas and education. In the first phase of the evaluation they installed our desktop indexer, then they chose three English language documents related to their everyday activities as follows:

- One *email* consisting of at least some sentences of written text, other than greetings;
- One *text document*, preferably text the user has written himself [7];
- One *web page* that would otherwise also be watched, saved directly from the internet.

The email and the text document were used in three forms, using only the beginning (min), an introductory part (med) or the whole document (max) as to simulate a work in progress and to be able to test the algorithm for his initial purpose, that of helping the user in completing his work. As the web page does not represent the work actually done by the user, this subdivision was not necessary, so only the full HTML body was used. This subdivision of the files would result in actually using seven different input file types - 3 email sizes (the first 5, 15 and all the sentences), 3 document sizes (the first 10, 25 and all the sentences) and 1 web page. The number of sentences used for simulating the user's work in progress is also presented in Table 3.8.

Each one of the three described algorithms was (1) first used only on the input file itself and (2) afterwards on the given file and other similar documents from the user's PC desktop. This results in a total of six used algorithms.

For each input file selected by the user the Top-5 results from Google API (as a software agent should not present the user with overwhelmingly too much informa-

---
[7] Usually, the researchers used articles for this task.

tion) generated by the 2 versions of the 3 algorithms we presented in Section 3.4.1, applied to 3 different file sizes for the email and the document and 1 for the web page (in total, 6 "algorithms" over 7 inputs, thus 42 result sets), were shuffled into one set so that the user was neither aware of the algorithm, nor of the ranking of each assessed URL . Thus, each subject had to assess about 170 URLs for three document types. Overall, 39 input files were selected and over 2,000 URLs were evaluated during the experiment. For each of these URLs, the testers had to give two marks ranging from 0 to 2 thus rating first the relevancy to the input file type as (0) not relevant, (1) relevant and (2) highly relevant; secondly they also rated the personal overall usefulness of the recommended web pages as (0) not useful at all, (1) useful and (2) very useful. The output quality was evaluated in terms of Mean Average Precision over the first 5 results (MAP@5) as well as precision at the first 1 through 5 positions of the resulted ranking (P@1 .. P@5). Finally, all our results were tested for statistical significance using T-tests (i.e., we tested whether the improvement over the simple intuitive Term Frequency algorithm output[8] is statistically significant).

Due to space limitations, for presenting the following result values we used a relaxed evaluation schema with regard to the marks given by the test subjects. Thus all the web links found to be relevant or highly relevant (marks 1 or 2) are treated as unitary. In fact, when using a strict evaluation, i.e. considering only highly relevant web links as relevant, the drawn conclusions are similar. More, when judging the usefulness of the web links with respect to the current user task, the relative performance of the algorithms with respect to each other remains mostly unchanged.

In all the forthcoming tables, we will use the following labeling:
- **TF**: The Term Frequency algorithm run on the input file only;
- **SS**: The Sentence Selection algorithm run on the input file only;
- **LC**: The Lexical Compounds algorithm run on the input file only;
- **TFD, SSD, LCD**: The previous three algorithms run on the input file and at most 10 similar files from the user's PC desktop;
- **Mail-5, Mail-15, Mail**: The first 5, 15, or all the sentences from the selected email;
- **Doc-10, Doc-25, Doc**: The first 10, 25, or all the sentences from the selected text document;
- **Web**: The entire selected web page.

Results

Email. The recall precision when searching for relevant web links to the current user task using an email as the input file type, with the three sizes the email was divided into, is presented graphically in Figures 3.3, 3.4, and 3.5. The three figures depict the

---
[8]Whenever necessary, we also tested for significance the difference between pairs of the algorithms we proposed.

3.4 Recommending Related Web Pages to User Tasks

precision, scaled from 0 to 1, as judged by the test subjects for all the five top links retrieved. We can see that although the average precision relies in the same interval for all the three email sizes, there are significant changes in the algorithms' performances. As the email grows bigger, the desktop compensation importance declines, because the user task can be more easily understood from the email itself. When considering only the first 5 sentences of an email, the algorithms show better results when applied over the desktop content also. For the first 15 sentences used, performances of the algorithms are similar, regardless of the extension over the desktop. As for the whole email, extending the user task with some general user profile keyword extracted from similar documents, usually yields poorer results.

From the algorithmic perspective, for the beginning of the email, the SSD and SS approaches show the best results, but as the email information increases, the precision for these algorithms is diminished, the lexical compound algorithms taking over. Although the precision is generally low, the SS and LC approaches show better results than TF without desktop, with LC at a significant level (p-value 0.02). Emails are usually very close related to the user personal interests, i.e. the user's desktop content; as a result, using the desktop usually brings an improvement, depending on the email size, especially with algorithms based on simpler statistics, such as TF.

Finally, we noticed that the recommended web results strongly depend on the location of the main topic words inside the email. When writing emails, users can get to the main point right after the greeting, or use some more sentences to describe a general situation or reply to some previous matter first. There are also often cases when replies also include the previous mail but have slight topic changes, where the users feel the main topic is the newer one, but the algorithms are not aware of the different topics contained, what results in extracting keywords of the same importance from throughout the whole email body. Usually the main topic of the email resides within the first 5 or 15 sentences, and therefore the precision slightly decreases on average as the email size increases. However, this cannot be generalized for every email. The best email description was extracted from the first 15 sentences, as only the first 5 include a lot of noise because of the introductory greeting typical to emails and except for very long emails, the email signature, usually present at the end of the email also adds significant noise. We are currently investigating more complex Topic Detection and Tracking (TDT) algorithms, which will allow us to better focus our keyword extraction algorithms towards the topically more relevant parts of each email.

Text Document. Results regarding the usage of a text document as the input file (Figures 3.6, 3.7, and 3.8) reveal that both Lexical Compounds methods (LC and LCD) yield the best results. Another important aspect ot note is that document size matters. In general, the bigger the document, the more relevant information should be available. However, for those subjects who used articles (may them be scientific, or news), utilizing the full-document contents resulted in slightly worse results than when considering only the first 10 or 25 sentences. This is because in such cases,

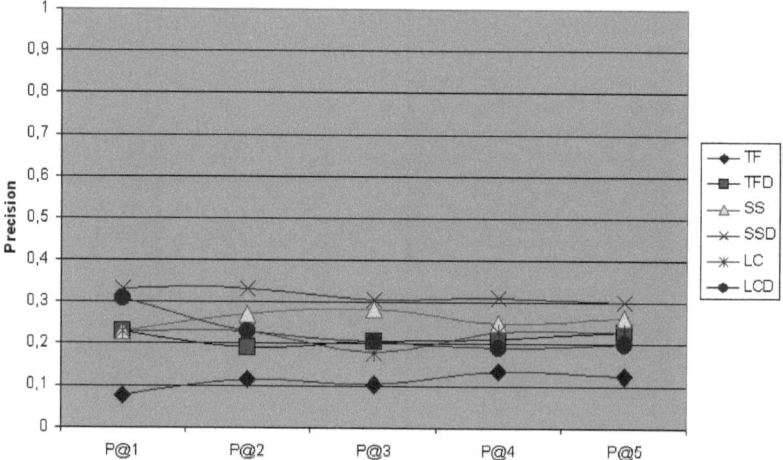

Figure 3.3 Precision at 1..5 considering only the first 5 sentences of an *email*

the first sentences abstract the entire text, and thus contain more topic-descriptive keywords than the rest of the document. For overall significance (the differences between all pairs of algorithms), p-value is 0.076, lowest for all input data. This is explainable, since manually edited documents contain both a personal language and enough interest-related words.

If only the currently active document is considered, then again the Lexical Compounds approach yields the best results, at a p-value of 0.097 versus TF. When this information is expanded with keywords extracted from other (similar) desktop documents, we observe a minimal loss of quality in the ratings, indicating that the active document provides a much clearer description of the current user task.

Web page. The results for the experiments with a web page as the input file type are depicted in Figure 3.9. Only the full text of the web page is considered as we do not simulate the user writing the web page step by step, but the user surfing the internet in search for knowledge.

The results show that the desktop supported keyword extraction variants usually produce results less precise than their single-document equivalents. This could be mainly because of differences in language use between local resources and global web pages. Although the simple term-frequency-based algorithm augmented by using similar desktop documents shows in this case the best performances overall, the statistical significance is not satisfied. Moreover, it is important to note that the desktop enhanced variants of our algorithms also require additional computation time, in order to analyze the desktop related documents. Thus though interesting from a theoretical

3.4 Recommending Related Web Pages to User Tasks

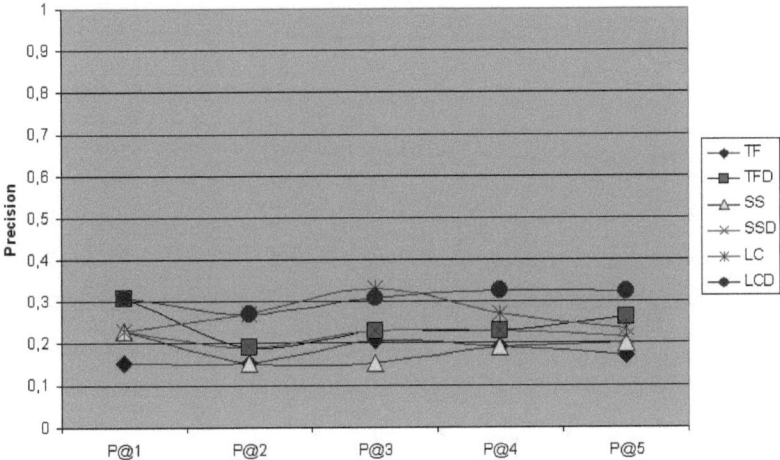

Figure 3.4 Precision at 1..5 considering only the first *15* sentences of an *email*

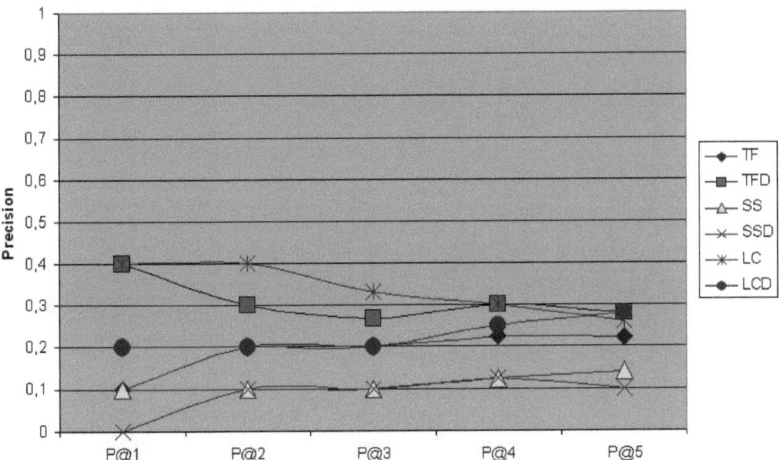

Figure 3.5 Precision at 1..5 considering the *entire* text of an *email*

perspective, they are less suitable for a real-life application, which should provide the web recommendations preferably within less than 1 second. When considering only

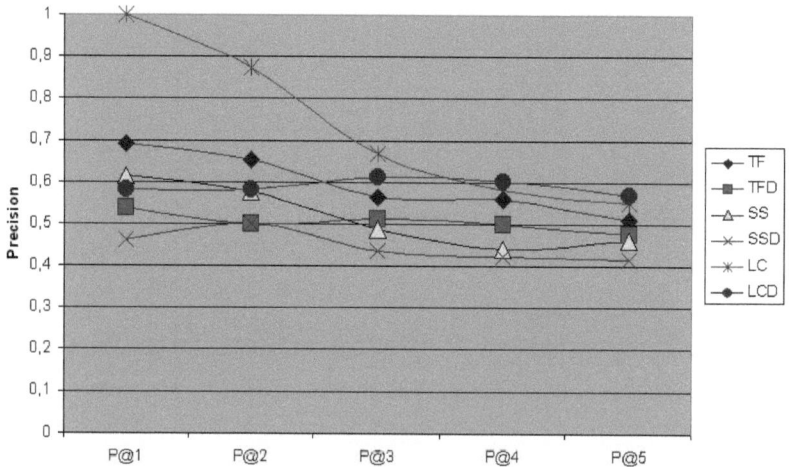

Figure 3.6 Precision at 1..5 considering only the first *10* sentences of a text *document*

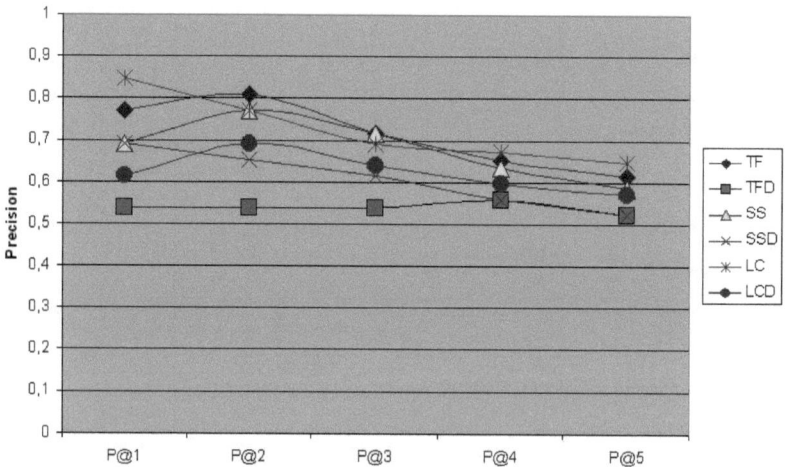

Figure 3.7 Precision at 1..5 considering only the first *25* sentences of a text *document*

3.4 Recommending Related Web Pages to User Tasks

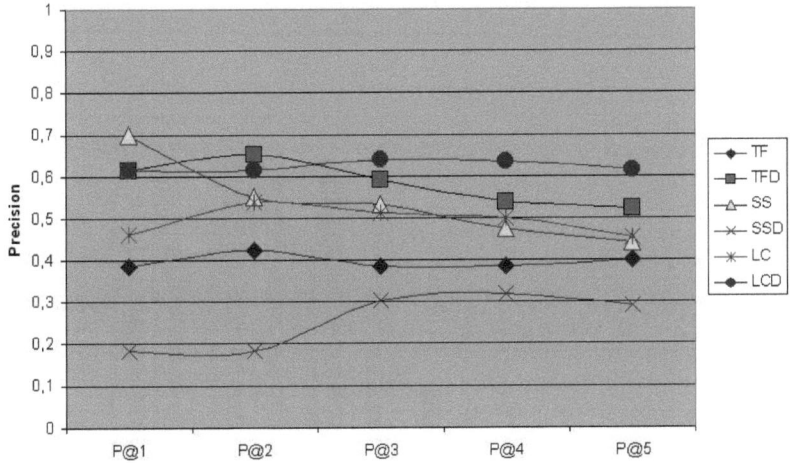

Figure 3.8 Precision at 1..5 considering the *entire* text *document*

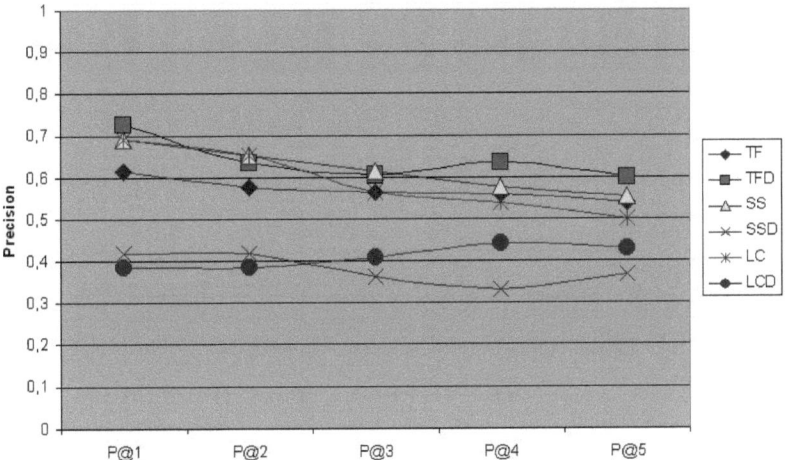

Figure 3.9 Precision at 1..5 considering the *entire* text of a *web page*

the current document, the *SS* approach performs best, followed by *LC*.

Overall Results. Like shown in Figure 3.10 and in Table 3.9, we can judge the usefulness of also including keywords from the desktop context in the query used to

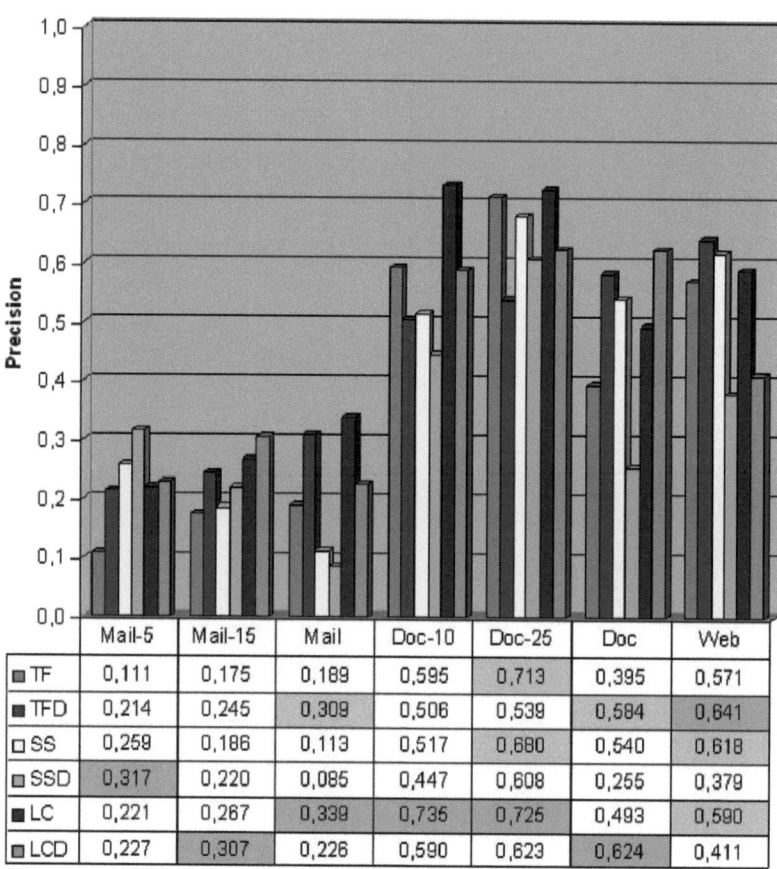

Figure 3.10 Mean average precision per input file type

Input type	TF	TFD	SS	SSD	LC	LCD
Email	0.158	**0.256**	0.186	0.207	**0.276**	**0.253**
Document	0.568	0.543	0.579	0.437	**0.651**	**0.612**
Web page	0.571	**0.641**	**0.618**	0.379	**0.590**	0.411

Table 3.9 Average precision for each algorithm per input file type

retrieve the relevant web links as very important. Using similar desktop documents improves precision, except for the cases when the whole document text or the web page is used as input. This is mainly due to desktop documents being too similar to the input file, in case of using the text document, or the desktop language differing from the web language in such a way that for a web page, the same syntactical structuring cannot be found in both the input file and the PC desktop. We also found the confirmation of our starting idea, that LC and SS perform better than the TF baseline, except for $Doc-10$ and $Doc-25$ where only LC performs better than TF. The explanation for this exception is that most of the used test input files were articles, where the first sentences are the paper abstract, and hence there is no need for further summarization.

Practical Issues. The response time is quite important for current search engines, and thus only those algorithms which can yield a quick valuable output are suitable for large scale topic independent applications. Therefore, even though the Sentence Selection approach did yield good results when used with context expansion techniques, as it is delayed by the computation of query specific sentence scores, it only makes a good candidate for domain specific search engines (e.g., medical), where some additional time can be traded for a better output. At the other end, both the Term Frequency and the Lexical Compounds methods provide very quick results, as their computation demanding step can be implemented off-line at indexing time, thus making them (especially the latter one) very suitable candidates for real world search applications. As the Lexical Compounds method resulted in the best precision scores, we think it is the best suited for recommending web pages in such a scenario.

3.5 Discussion

Textual Web IR has reached a stage where few improvements in ranking or retrieval effectiveness are foreseeable. The focus lies more on result presentation and on ranking personalization. We have shown in this chapter such personalization algorithms using the most valuable source of information about a user – all personal resources on the Desktop – as well as different applications.

In Section 3.2 we proposed Query Clarity as an indicator of user's search reformulation actions, and showed it to be more flexible than traditional approaches, which build onto naïve instruments such as the number of keywords. Moreover, we also analyzed the Part-Of-Speech transition patterns over a large search engine log.

Building upon the query reformulation analysis, in Section 3.3 we proposed to expand Web search queries by exploiting the user's Personal Information Repository in order to automatically extract additional keywords related both to the query itself and to user's interests, personalizing the search output. In this context, the section includes the following contributions: We proposed five techniques for determining expansion terms from personal documents. Each of them produces additional query keywords by analyzing user's Desktop at increasing granularity levels, ranging from term and expression level analysis up to global co-occurrence statistics and external thesauri. We provided a thorough empirical analysis of several variants of our approaches, under four different scenarios. We showed some of these approaches to perform very well, producing NDCG improvements of up to 51.28%. We moved this personalized search framework further and proposed to make the expansion process adaptive to features of each query, a strong focus being put on its clarity level. Within a separate set of experiments, we showed our adaptive algorithms to provide an additional improvement of 8.47% over the previously identified best approach.

We then (Section 3.4) proposed another application of the personalization algorithms: extract keywords from the user's active documents in order to describe the current user task, and present personalized recommendations. The approaches, Sentence Selection and Lexical Compounds, adapt summarization and natural language processing techniques to extract these keywords from the active document or additionally from locally stored desktop documents. We investigated the performance of these with respect to three types of input files, namely emails, text documents and web pages. Our experiments showed an improvement over the baseline in Mean Average Precision of 18% for the SS approach and 41% for the LC approach, with a maximum improvement of 187% of the SSD algorithm over the TF method when using only the first 5 sentences of an email as input. The results show that using good text extraction techniques always improves over a simple baseline, for all input file types. Moreover, using additional information from related documents improves effectiveness regardless of the algorithm.

4

Automatic Semantic Enrichment

4.1 Introduction

We have seen in the previous chapter how personalization effectively increases Precision. The complementary measure of perceived user satisfaction in IR, Recall, can be increased by enriching data with additional annotations. Especially for resources where textual information is very restricted, as is the case of audio-visual resources, providing an as-complete-as-possible representation of a resource is essential. As extraction of audio and visual features directly from the resources is still emerging from the performance point of view, a very significant source of textual information is provided by user generated annotations.

Collaborative tagging as a flexible means for information organization and sharing has become highly popular in recent years. By assigning freely selectable words to bookmarked Web pages (*Del.icio.us*), to music (*Last.fm*) or pictures (*Flickr*) users generate a huge amount of semantically rich metadata. Consequently, several well known tagging systems have been acquired by search engine companies to exploit this additional information during search. Especially for multimedia resources, accurate annotations are extremely useful, as these additional textual descriptions can be used to support multimedia retrieval.

Still, users' motivations for tagging, as well as the types of assigned tags differ across systems, and despite initial investigations, their potential to improve search remains unclear. What kinds of tags are used, and which types can improve search most? We investigate this issue in detail in Section 4.2, by analyzing tag data from three very different tagging systems: *Del.icio.us*, *Flickr* and *Last.fm*. Our comparative study of the users' tagging and querying habits reveals some interesting aspects. While in general tag and query distributions have similar characteristics, some significant differences are to be noted: usage (*theme*) is very prevalent in user queries for music as well as opinion (*mood*) concepts for music and pictures queries, but many more tags of these types would be needed.

Prior studies, which started to investigate users' motivations for tagging and the resulting nature of such user provided annotations, discovered that both motivations for tagging, as well as the types of assigned tags differ quite a lot across systems. However, not all tags are equally useful for search. For example, a user might tag a picture on *Flickr* with some of the things depicted on it, like "flowers", "sun", "nature", or with the associated location ("London") and time ("2008"). Since such tags are factual in nature, i.e. they are verifiable at least by common sense, they are potentially relevant to all other users searching for pictures e.g. from this location. However, to provide some more context for sharing her images with friends, she may also add more subjective, contextual tags like "awesome" or "post-graduate trip", or she may refer to herself by using the annotation "my friends". Assuming a certain amount of interpersonal agreement, subjective tags may still be useful for some users. For the majority of users, the tag "awesome" for example, may be an indicator of the quality of the picture, but not for people disagreeing with popular opinion. Self reference tags on the other hand are so highly personal that another person may not understand the tag at all or associate something different with it (e.g. her own post-graduate trip to Asia). Thus, personal tags are not applicable to other users of the system, except from the user herself and maybe some of her friends. Still, for estimating similarity between resources or users search engines and recommendation algorithms exploiting user generated annotations but not differentiating types of tags and their interpersonal value incorporate all (frequent) tags and thus introduce noise. Being able to distinguish between the types of tags associated to resources would thus be highly beneficial for search engines and recommendation algorithms to best support users in their information needs. Besides, tag classes enable building enhanced navigation tools. While currently the user faces a potentially infinite, unordered tag space, tag classes would allow for browsing pictures, web sites or music by the different informational facets of the associated tags.

The findings of the analysis are essential, especially for the case of tagging systems focusing mostly on multimedia resources. While for Web pages or publications, tags may not improve retrieval that much, for pictures, music or movies the gain is substantial. Content-based retrieval is still not mature enough to enable scalable content-based search. Moreover, even with the most prominent search engines on the Web today, users are still constrained to search for music or pictures using textual queries. In this context, supporting users in providing meaningful tags for this type of resources becomes crucial.

One possibility to make users use keywords from the categories we need is to unobtrusively recommend such tags and thus support them in the tagging process. Beside minimizing the cognitive load by changing the task from generation to recognition [SOHB07], such recommendation of under-represented but valuable tags will very likely trigger reinforcement, i.e. enforce preferential attachment. As presented in [SLR+06, HRS07], seeing previous tag assignments from other users strongly influences which tags will be assigned next and thus to which tag set a resource's

4.1 Introduction

vocabulary will converge.

We build upon results of previous studies [BFNP08, BFNP09, BFP09a], and propose algorithms relying on tags for identifying other types of valuable knowledge about music and picture resources in Section 4.3. We propose a novel approach for detecting emotions in photos relying on collaborative tagging, state-of-the-art solutions being content based. With the presented algorithms we manage to bridge some significant gaps in the tagging and querying vocabularies, thus enabling more efficient multimedia information retrieval – extensive experiments demonstrate the performance of the proposed algorithms and compare their results against baseline algorithms.

The methods we propose can be used in various ways: as part of an application where the recommendations are presented directly to the user, who can select the relevant ones and add them to the item that is currently annotated. Another possibility is to index the recommended mood and theme tags, thus enriching the metadata indexes. Last but not least, the recommendations can be used to automatically create mood or theme-based playlists in case of music resources, or mood-based picture catalogs.

Going further in the evolution of Web 2.0 sites, we shift our focus towards representation and management of multimedia resources as events. We define an event like in [tdt], as a specific thing happening at a specific time and place. Moreover, we consider events having both a local and a global dimension. Events such as birthdays, a marriage, a summer vacation or a car accident are the lens through which we see and memorize our own personal experiences and are therefore events of local type. In turn, global events, such as world sport championships or global natural disasters (e.g. 2010 Haiti earthquake, 2004 Thailand tsunami, climate change, world recession, etc.) or, on a smaller scale, a local festival or a soccer match, build collective experiences. These types of events allow users share personal experiences as a part of a more social phenomenon – "collective events".

The key idea of Section 4.4 is to use events as the primary means to organize media and in a more concrete scenario, pictures. Our lives are a constellation of events, which one after another, pace our everyday activities and build up our memories. Many of the *Flickr* pictures have been shot during specific events, therefore enabling users to organize or browse this type of media by events is very natural.

Users often do not invest much effort in organizing their own pictures and prefer instead to create quite broad sets including hundreds of pictures. Because of this, a huge amount of digital pictures remains untouched unless powerful techniques for image retrieval become available. Image retrieval is particularly difficult, given the fact that *Flickr* data is noisy and, besides, it is not easy to capture the content of photos. Our approach for classifying pictures into events relies entirely on user provided annotations, which we gather from the *Flickr* Web site. The extensive automatic evaluations we perform demonstrate the high accuracy of our algorithms. Moreover, the applicability of the methods we introduce is not restricted to pictures in *Flickr*, but can be employed for any types of pictures having tags associated with them, as well as to other types of multimedia data, e.g. videos, music, etc. Additionally, the methods can be applied not only for event-based browsing or organization, but also for enabling users to discover other users interested in the same types of events and thus easing social connectivity.

4.2 Analysis of Tag Usage

Collaborative tagging has become an increasingly popular means for sharing and organizing Web resources, leading to a huge amount of user generated metadata. These annotations represent quite a few different aspects of the resources they are attached to, but it is not obvious which characteristics of the objects are predominantly described. The usefulness of these tags for finding / re-finding the annotated resources is also not completely clear. Several studies have started to investigate these issues, however only by focusing on a single type of tagging system or resource. We study this problem across multiple domains and resource types and identify the gaps between the tag space and the querying vocabulary. Based on the findings of this analysis, we then try to bridge the identified gaps, focusing in particular on multimedia resources.

The following section presents and discusses the results of our comparative investigations of tag usage in *Last.fm*, *Del.icio.us*, and *Flickr*. Looking at the usage of different types of tags, we first identify and quantify the distinctions occurring in users' tagging behavior. Most of the tags are potentially useful for search, though not all kinds of tags are equally valuable. We then investigate how well users' tagging and searching behaviors correspond.

4.2.1 Data Set Descriptions

Last.fm. For our analysis, we have crawled an extensive subset of the *Last.fm* website in May 2007, focusing on pages corresponding to tags, music tracks and user profiles. We obtained information about a total number of 317,058 tracks and their associated attributes, including track and artist name, as well as tags for these tracks plus their corresponding usage frequencies. Starting from the most popular tags, we found a number of 21,177 different tags, which are used on *Last.fm* for tagging tracks, artists or albums. For each of these tags we extracted the number of times each tag has been used, number of users which used the tag, as well as lists of similar tags.

Flickr. For comparison with *Flickr* characteristics, we took advantage of data crawled by our research partners during January 2004 and December 2005. The crawling was done by starting with some initial tags from the most popular ones and then expanding the crawl based on these tags. We used a small portion of the first 100,000 pictures crawled, associated with 32,378 unique tags assigned with different frequencies.

Del.icio.us. The *Del.icio.us* data for our analysis was also kindly provided by

4.2 Analysis of Tag Usage

research partners. This data was collected during July 2005 by gathering a first set of nearly 6,900 users and 700 tags from the start page of *Del.icio.us*. These were used to download more data in a recursive manner. Additional users and resources were collected by monitoring the *Del.icio.us* start page. A list of several thousands usernames was collected and used for accessing the first 10,000 resources each user had tagged. From the collected data we extracted resources, tags, dates, descriptions, usernames, etc. The resulting collection comprises 323,294 unique tags associated with 2,507,688 bookmarks.

Usage of tags basically follows a power law distribution for each system. The most evenly distributed system is *Flickr*, where people almost always tag only their own pictures, not much influenced by others. For *Del.icio.us*, influence of others is more visible: popular tags are being used more often, while tags in the tail have less weight. *Last.fm* has even fewer very popular tags, 60% of the top 100 representing genre information. Since *Last.fm* covers a very specific domain tags are more restricted than in *Flickr*, where images can include everything and in *Del.icio.us*, which has an even broader range of topics.

In order to improve tag based search, we first need to know how tags are used and which types of annotations we can expect to find along with resources. To make intellectual analysis feasible we had to sample our data, we manually investigated 900 tags in total. For the three different tagging systems, we took three samples of 100 tags each to be manually classified based on a tag type taxonomy presented in Section 4.2.2. These three samples per system included the top 100 tags, 100 tags starting from 70% of probability density (based on absolute occurrences), and 100 tags beginning from 90%. These different samples based on rank percentages were chosen based on the results of prior work [HRS07] which suggested that different parts of the power law curve exhibit distinct patterns.

Like for other complex systems patterns evolve in collaborative tagging systems that follow a scale-free power law distribution, indicating convergence of the used vocabulary coexisting with a long tail of highly idiosyncratic terms [HRS07, HJSS06]. Commonly used, more general tags have higher proportions [GH06]. Possible explanations are the imitation of other users' behavior, shared knowledge [GH06] and preferential attachment [HRS07] as well as effects of system design choices [SLR$^+$06, MNBD06]. Halpin et al. [HRS07] relate this to the principle of least efforts: While speakers prefer ambiguous, general terms, hearers prefer words with high entropy. Thus, the conflict arises between taggers agreeing to a convention or accepting the need for complex, multiple queries. The folksonomy structure evolves due to the consensus arising when tagging, even though tagging is mostly for personal benefit. Our goal here is to provide descriptive statistics about tag type usage depending on popularity.

Nr.	Category	Last.fm	Flickr	Del.icio.us
1	Topic	romance, revolution	people, flowers	webdesign, linux
2	Time	80s	2005, july	daily, current
3	Location	england, african	toronto, kingscross	slovakia, newcastle
4	Type	pop, acoustic	portrait, 50mm	movies, mp3, blogs
5	Author/Owner	the beatles, wax trax	wright	wired, alanmoore
6	Opinions/Qualities	great lyrics, rowdy	scary, bright	annoying, funny
7	Usage context	workout, study, lost	vacation, science	review.later, travelling
8	Self reference	albums i own, seen live	me, 100views	frommyrssfeeds

Table 4.1 Tag classification taxonomy, applicable to different tagging systems

4.2.2 Tags' Characteristics

Defining Tag Types

For the purpose of analysing the kinds of tags used in collaborative tagging, we propose and use an extended tag taxonomy suitable for different tagging systems. We started with an exploratory analysis of existing taxonomies (see [GH06, SLR+06, XFMS06]), as well as possible attribute fields for the different resources to be considered. We kept and refined the most fine-grained scheme presented by Golder and Huberman [GH06], adding the classes *Time* and *Location*, in order to make it applicable to systems other than *Del.icio.us*, which only focuses on Web page annotations. We went through several iterations to improve the scheme by classifying sample tags and testing for agreement between multiple raters. Our final taxonomy comprises eight classes, presented together with example tags from our datasets in Table 4.1.

Topic is probably the most obvious way to describe an arbitrary resource, referring to what a tagged item is about. For music, *Topic* was defined to include main subject (e.g. "romance"), title and lyrics. The *Topic* of a picture refers to any object or person displayed. While such *Topic* information can partially be extracted from the content of textual resources [HKGM08], it is not easily accessible for pictures or music. Tags in the *Time* category add contextual information about month, year, season, or other time related modifiers. This includes the time a picture was taken, a music piece or Web page was produced. Similarly, *Location* is an additional retrieval cue, providing information about sights, country or town, or the origin of a musician. Tags may also specify the *Type*, which mainly corresponds to file, media or Web page type ("pdf",

4.2 Analysis of Tag Usage

"blog", etc.). In music this category comprises tags specifying encoding as well as instrumentation and music genre. For pictures, this includes camera settings and photographic styles like "portrait" or "macro". Yet another way to organize resources is by identifying the *Author/Owner* who created the resource (author, artist) or owns it (a music and entertainment group like Sony BMG or a *Flickr* user). Tags can also comment subjectively on the quality of a resource (*Opinions/Qualities*), expressing opinions based on social motivations typical for free-for-all-tagging systems, or are simply used as rating-like annotations to ease personal retrieval. *Usage context* tags suggest what to use a resource for, or the context/task the resource was collected in and grouped by. These tags (e.g. "jobsearch", "forProgramming", etc.), although subjective, may still be a good basis for recommendations to other users. Last, *Self reference* contains highly personal tags, mostly helpful for the tagger herself.

Clearly, such classification schemes only represent one possible way of categorizing things. Quite a few tags are ambiguous due to homonymy (especially for *Flickr* and *Del.icio.us*, e.g. "apple"). Here, we based our decision on the most popular resource(s) tagged. During classification we even found some tags considered as 'factual' difficult to classify directly. For example, "vacation" can be considered as the Topic of a Web resource, as well as a personal tag of type Usage context grouping resources for the next holidays. Similarly "zoo" or "festival" may be depicted in a picture or used as context attributes not directly inferable from the resource. Depending on the intended usage as well as probably subjective and cultural differences such tags fit into more than one category. This problem of concise category boundaries also applies to the other categorization schemes presented in related work.

For evaluating our scheme using inter-rater agreement, we selected 75 tags per system from our initial sample (25 randomly chosen tags per popularity range) and had it assessed by students unfamiliar with the tag categorization scheme. We computed Cohen's unweighted Kappa (κ) [Coh60] which aims at indicating the achieved inter-rater agreement beyond-chance, as the standard measure to assess concordance for our nominal data. Our raw agreement value for the κ calculation is about 0.79 given the sum of 0.77 for the by chance expected frequencies, resulting in a κ of 0.71. This is considered substantial inter-rater reliability [LK77]. Part of the disagreement observed may be caused by ambiguity of the classification scheme. The confusion matrix created for the κ calculation reveals several prominent confusion patterns for the *Del.icio.us* tags always involving the default *Topic* category. Specifically, in several cases we found disagreement on whether a tag indicated the *Topic* or *Type*, *Author/Owner* or *Usage context*. These may indicate fuzzy category boundaries or/and subjectivity and cultural dependency, showing the direction of further improvements. To account for the ambiguity in tag meaning and tag function for certain resources, we gave the rater a chance to name a second category that would fit as well. Taking into account this second possible category for a tag, our κ improved considerably to 0.80.

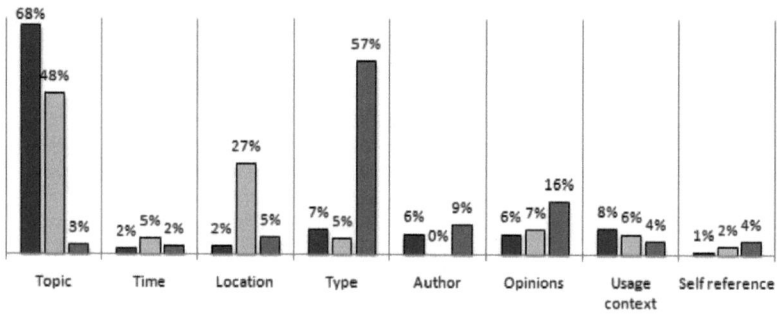

Figure 4.1 Tag type distributions across systems

Distribution of Tag Types Across Systems

Having defined this general tag taxonomy, we are interested in seeing the tag distributions over the eight tag classes. We classified all sample tags taken from the three different systems according to the established taxonomy. The resulting distributions of tag types across systems are shown in Figure 4.1[1]. A general conclusion is that tag types are very different for different collections. Specifically, the most important category for *Del.icio.us* and *Flickr* is *Topic*, while for *Last.fm*, the *Type* category is the most prominent one, due to the abundance of genre tags, which fall into this class. Obviously, genre is the easiest way of characterizing and organizing music. One of the rare exceptions was for the theme "romance" and some parts of the lyrics or title. In contrast, a similar dominance can be observed for *Topic* in case of Web resources and pictures. *Type* is also common in *Del.icio.us*, as it specifies whether a page contains certain media. As *Flickr* is used only for pictures, *Type* variations only include fine grained distinctions like "macro", but most users do not seem to make such professional annotations. For pictures only, *Location* plays an important role. *Usage context* seems to be more used in *Del.icio.us* and *Flickr*, while *Last.fm* as a free-for-all-tagging system (with lower motivation for organization) exhibits a significantly higher amount of subjective (*Opinions/Qualities*) tags. *Time* and *Self reference* only represent a very small part of the tags studied here. *Author/Owner* is a little more frequent, though very rarely used in *Flickr* due to the fact that people mainly tag their own pictures [MNBD06].

Studying the the distributions for all systems across all samples, we find that the

---

[1]In later work, we classified 700 sample tags per tagging system, resulting in similar distributions [BFK+09]

4.2 Analysis of Tag Usage

type distribution between systems shows a clear tendency of preferred tag functions that do not depend much on the popularity of the tags.

With respect to exploiting tags in web search, it is encouraging to see, that most tags are factual in nature, verifiable and thus potentially relevant to the community and other users. This applies to *Topics* and resource *Type* in general, *Topic* and *Location* for pictures, and to a certain degree *Type* for music. Subjective and personal tags (categories 6, 8) are only a minor part. Similar to results reported in [Zol07], *Opinions/Qualities* are only characteristic for social, free-for-all music tagging systems (like *Last.fm*), possibly because for young people (exposing) music taste is one important aspect in forming one's own personal identity.

Other interesting results of this analysis refer to the added value of tags to existing content: More than 50% of existing tags bring new information to the resources they annotate. From the *Del.icio.us* crawl we had extracted 20,911 URLs for which we had the full HTML page[2]. For these we counted how many tags appear in the Web page text they annotate and found that this is the case for 44.85% of the selected *Del.icio.us* tags. In the music domain this is even the case for 98.5% of the tags as *Last.fm* tags are usually not contained at all in lyrics (the only textual original content available). For a subsample of 77,498 tracks, we took all tags corresponding to the tracks and tried to find them in the track lyrics. The curve follows a power law distribution. On average, 1.54% of the tracks' tags occurred in the lyrics. Especially for multimedia data, such as music, pictures or videos, the gain provided by the newly available textual information is substantial.

We also showed that a large amount of tags is accurate and reliable; in the music domain, for example, 73.01% of the tags also occur in online music reviews retrieved by Google, 46.14% are even to be found in expert reviews on *AllMusic.com*. To analyze the overlap between tags assigned to *Last.fm* tracks and music reviews extracted from Google results, we randomly selected 8,130 tracks from our original dataset, for which we tried to find music reviews by sending queries in the form [*"artist" "track" music review -lyrics*] to Google. The same query was used in [KPSW07]. For each of the selected tracks we considered the top 100 Google results, and extracted the text of the corresponding pages to create one single document inside which we searched for the tags corresponding to the track. The tag distribution found was linear and 73.01% of the track tags occurred inside review pages. This overlap is rather high, and probably caused by the fact that most of the *Last.fm* tags represent genre names, which also occur very often in music reviews.

Second, we investigated how many of the tags assigned to tracks occurred in the manually created expert reviews from *AllMusic.com*. We randomly selected music tracks from our *Last.fm* dataset and crawled the Web pages corresponding to their *AllMusic.com* reviews. If no review was available for one track, we tried to find the review Web page of the album featuring that track. The resulting dataset consisted

---

[2]The HTML pages were taken from a WebBase crawl (http://dbpubs.stanford.edu:8091/~testbed/doc2/WebBase/)

78   Chapter 4 Automatic Semantic Enrichment

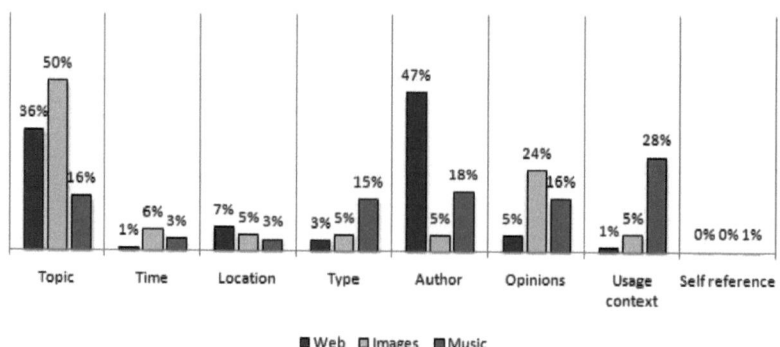

Figure 4.2 Distribution of query types for different resources

of 3,600 reviews. Following the same procedure as for the previous experiment with reviews retrieved via Google, we found that 46.14% of the tags belonging to a track occurred on the *AllMusic.com* review pages. Again the tag distribution we found is linear. We hypothesize that the lower number of matches is due to the fact that *AllMusic.com* reviews are created by a relatively small number of human experts, which use a more homogeneous and thus restricted vocabulary than found in arbitrary reviews on the Web. Still, at least one *Last.fm* tag occurs in the review texts for almost all analyzed tracks. This proves tags to be a reliable source of metadata about songs, created more easily by a much higher number of users.

4.2.3 Usefulness of Tags for Search

Extending and complementing our tagging analysis, we also explored how users' searching and tagging behavior compare. In this experiment, we investigated how much current Web queries overlap with tags. We used the AOL query logs [PCT06] to calculate the overlap between Web queries and tags, and contrasted tag and query classes. In our comparative analysis of tags and queries we tried to map web queries onto the tag taxonomy established in Section 4.2.2, thus investigating which kind of tags could best answer a given query. We built a frequency sorted list of all queries in the AOL log and took three samples from different regions of the power law curves. We sampled 300 queries per type of resource (images, songs, Web pages), by filtering the query log for queries containing a keyword (like "music", "song", "picture", etc.) or having a click on *Last.fm* or *Flickr*. The resulting queries were classified into our eight categories, with queries belonging to multiple classes in case they consisted of terms corresponding to different functions.

4.2 Analysis of Tag Usage

The results are shown in Figure 4.2. Not quite surprisingly, general Web queries often name the *Topic* of a resource, just like tags in *Del.icio.us* do to an even larger extent. The query distribution pattern fits to distributions of tags except for a clear difference regarding category 5 (*Author/Owner*). *Usage context* is more often used for tag based information organization than for search. For obvious reasons, *Self reference* is not a useful query type for public Web resources.

For images, our tag type distribution almost perfectly corresponds to the query type patterns. As Figure 4.2 shows, *Topic* accounts for about half of the queries, as well as of the tags in *Flickr*. Slight differences exist for *Location*, used more for tagging than for searching and *Author/Owner* being somewhat more important for queries than for tagging. Interestingly, there seem to be many more subjective queries asking for *Opinions/Qualities* like "funny", "public" or "sexy" pictures. With decreasing popularity of tags, this category becomes somewhat less important, but prevalence of *Topic* and *Location* increases. While the number of 'adult content' queries in picture search was high for all three subsamples of varying popularity, this kind of tags was completely underrepresented in our analysed samples of *Flickr*, *Del.icio.us* and *Last.fm* (one tag in *Del.icio.us*)[3].

The biggest deviation between queries and tags occurs for music queries. While our tags in *Last.fm* are to a large extent genre names, user queries often belong to the *Usage context* category (like "wedding songs" or songs from a movie, category 7). Also, users search for known music by artist (category 5), title or theme (category 1). These differences may be due to information value considerations: as artist and title are already provided in *Last.fm* as formal metadata there is no need to tag resources with this information. Lyrics are not frequently searched for. A surprising observation is that searching by genre is rare: Users intensively use tags from this category, but do not use them to search for music. One reason for this might be that many music pieces get tagged with the same genre and thus search results for genre queries would contain far too many hits. Categorizing tracks into genre is also subjective to a certain extent, as it depends on the annotator's expertise. The amount of subjective qualities asked for or tagged is comparable for the *Last.fm* system, with 16% each.

Comparing categories of tags and queries offers some interesting insights: Most of the general Web queries are *Topic*-related queries (as most of the tags for *Del.icio.us* and *Flickr*). For Web resources *Topic* tags are very useful, as over 30% of the queries target this category; but we also see that although users query the *Author/Owner* category, they usually do not tag in this way. For images, the *Topic* category is as prominent and important for tags as it is for queries. However, many queries are about *Opinions/Qualities* but users tend to add more *Location* tags than the needed *Opinions/Qualities*. So, even if users actually like to search for "funny" or "scary" pictures, they often do not tag them in this way. As for the music domain, tags generally fall into the *Type* (i.e. genres) class, although more tags from *Usage context*

---
[3]this holds also for the larger sample analysed in [BFK+09]

and *Topic* categories would be needed (*Author/Owner* is already present). This leads to the necessity of providing ways to extend and direct the tagging vocabulary towards the sought classes.

4.3 Knowledge Discovery Through Tags

We have shown in the previous sections how different types of tags exhibit different levels of usefulness, and that some tag types which are particularly useful in the search scenario are underrepresented as user generated metadata. Semantically rich user generated annotations are especially valuable for multimedia resources, where these metadata enable retrieval relying not only on content-based (low-level) features, but also on the textual descriptions represented by tags. We focus on the two scenarios of music and picture resources and develop algorithms, which identify usage (*theme*) and opinion (*mood*) characteristics of the items. The mood and theme labels our algorithms infer are recommended to the users, in order to support them during the annotation process. The evaluation of the proposed methods against user judgments, as well as against expert ground truth reveal the high quality of our recommended annotations and provide insights into possible extensions for music and picture tagging systems to support retrieval.

In the previous sections we have seen that tags are in general very useful for search applications. Nevertheless, in some cases we could identify some clear gaps between the tagging and querying vocabulary: *Usage context* for music and *Opinion* for both music and picture resources. Here, many more tags from these categories would be needed for supporting the very frequent queries targeting such characteristics of the content.

In order to bridge these gaps in the tagging vocabulary, we propose solutions based on tags. The semantically rich user generated annotations are especially valuable for content collections covering multimedia resources such as music, pictures or video items, where these metadata enable retrieval relying not only on content-based (low-level) features, but also on the textual descriptions represented by tags. Apart from being extremely important for multimedia retrieval, tags can also reveal some of the hidden aspects of the content they annotate, and which would be much more expensive to extract through content analysis methods. In turn, these hidden content features that are made accessible through either tag or content analysis, can be used to support information retrieval.

For example, in case of music resources, tags reveal a lot more information than only the music genre a track belongs to. They can for instance indicate which is the emotional state induced by listening to a particular song (e.g. happy, sad, lazy, aggressive, etc.) or which is the most suitable situation for listening to some music (e.g. pool party, wedding, rainy day, dinner ambiance, driving, etc.). Similarly, tags attached to picture resources can reveal both simple information, such as names of

4.3 Knowledge Discovery Through Tags

persons appearing on the photos, location names, or personal impressions regarding the event where the picture has been taken, etc., as well as more complex information, such as users' opinions regarding the objects depicted on the photos (e.g. scary, funny, etc.). Having music and picture items indexed also according to these features will advance considerably current possibilities of multimedia search and retrieval.

In this section we will thus focus on inferring additional information from the tags associated with music and picture resources and recommend it to the users during the annotation process. This way we support users in providing tags from the categories we need. More specifically, we will develop methods to identify the corresponding "moods" and "themes" for songs, as well as pictures' "moods". With "mood" we understand the state or quality of a particular feeling induced by listening to a particular songs / seeing a particular photo (e.g. *aggressive, happy, sad, funny*, etc.). The "theme" of a song refers to the context or situation which best fits for listening to songs (e.g. *at the beach, dinner ambiance, night driving, party time*, etc.).

4.3.1 Data Set Descriptions

To obtain the datasets for our experiments we used several data sources: *Last.fm*, *AllMusic.com*, www.lyricsdownload.com, www.lyricsmode.com and *Flickr*. In the following we present some relevant statistics for all of them.

AllMusic.com (**AM**). Established in 1995, the *AllMusic.com* website was created as a place and community for music fans. Not only all genres can be found on *AllMusic.com*, but also reviews of albums and artists within the context of their own genres, as well as classifications of songs and albums according to themes, moods or instruments. All these reviews and classifications are manually created by music experts from the *AllMusic.com* team, therefore the data found here serves as a good ground truth corpus. For our experiment we collected the *AllMusic.com* pages corresponding to music themes and moods; we could find 178 different moods and 73 themes. From the pages corresponding to moods/themes, we also gathered information related to which music tracks fall into these categories and we restrict the dataset to contain only tracks also present in our *Last.fm* crawl.

Last.fm (**LFM**). For the purpose of our investigations, we crawled an extensive subset of the *Last.fm* website, namely pages corresponding to tags, music tracks and user profiles. We started from the crawl described in Section 4.2.1 and recollected the information related to tags associated with music tracks. From all tracks that we obtained from *AllMusic.com*, we could also find 13,948 of them in the *Last.fm* dataset. For this intersection we had 81,964 different tags and for each of these tags we have extracted information regarding the number of times each tag has been used.

Lyrics (**LY**). To investigate whether another source of information, namely lyrics, as one part of music content, can provide added value in the task of mood and theme recommendation, we also obtained the corresponding lyrics for our tracks, if available. Here, we used a previous crawl (described in [BFNP08]) of the www.lyricsdownload.

com site. Additionally, we crawled the www.lyricsmode.com website, such that we could gather the lyrics for a total of 6,915 tracks.

Flickr (**F**). For the purpose of deriving mood labels for pictures, we collected data from *Flickr* using its API[4]. We started by manually selecting *Flickr* groups that correspond to the emotion/mood labels we wanted to predict, and more explicitly, we made use of the hierarchy of human emotions presented in Table 4.2. We could find corresponding *Flickr* groups for 17 out of the 25 secondary emotions, including the six primary emotion labels as well. For all identified groups we downloaded all associated metadata, in particular the user assigned tags, for all pictures contained in this group.

4.3.2 Deriving Music Moods and Themes

As we could see in Section 4.2, the majority of tags associated with music resources corresponds to genre information (around 60% of the tags). This is somehow redundant information, as it can also be extracted from ID3 tags. Considerably less frequent are tags referring to moods (20%) or themes (5%), though when searching for music, the majority of queries falls into these categories: 30% of the queries are theme-related, 15% target mood information and the rest being almost uniformly distributed among six other categories. A natural question that arises is therefore: How can we support users to provide these kinds of tags? Consider for example the song of ABBA, "Dancing Queen": by listening to the song or just considering the lyrics (*"Friday night and the lights are low / looking out for the place to go / where they play the right music / getting in the swing ..."*) one immediately gets transposed into a weekend party atmosphere and an enjoyable state of mind. It would therefore be natural to describe and also search for this song with mood related words such as "fun", "happy", etc. and with theme tags like "Party Time", "Thank God It's Friday!" or "Girls Night Out". Nevertheless, when inspecting the tags *Last.fm* users provided for this track, we cannot really identify these concepts. Instead, tags such as "pop", "disco", "70s" or "dance" are quite often employed. With the algorithms we describe in this section we can provide users with mood- and theme-related tags to choose from during the tagging process and we use the **AM**, **LFM** and **LY** datasets introduced in Section 4.3.1.

Music Mood and Theme Recommendation Algorithm

To recommend themes and moods, we base our solution on collaboratively created social knowledge, i.e. tags associated with music tracks, extracted from *Last.fm*, as well as on lyrics information. Based on already provided user tags, on the lyrics of music tracks, or on combinations of the two, we build classifiers which try to infer

---
[4] http://www.flickr.com/services/api/

4.3 Knowledge Discovery Through Tags

other annotations corresponding to the moods and themes of the songs. Our approach thus relies on the following hypotheses:

1. Existing tags provided by users for a particular song carry information which can be used to infer the mood or theme of that song, e.g. songs tagged with "hard-rock" are more likely to have an "aggressive" mood than "mellow"-tagged songs.

2. The lyrics of the tracks give a hint on the mood or theme of the songs. For example, tracks with love-related lyrics have "romantic evening" as theme and correspondingly, a "romantic" mood.

In order to recommend mood and theme annotations we thus build probabilistic classifiers trained on the *AllMusic.com* ground truth using tags and/or lyrics as features. Separate classifiers correspond to the different types of classes that we aim to recommend and to build the classifiers, we use the open source machine learning library Weka[5]. In the experiments presented, we use the Naïve Bayes Multinomial implementation. Several other classifiers (e.g. Support Vector Machines, Decision Trees) have been tested, which resulted in similar classification performances, but were much more computationally intensive. We have one classifier trained for the whole available set of classes (i.e. either for moods or themes) and this classifier produces for every song in the test set a probability distribution over all classes (e.g. over all moods). Thus, one or more classes (based on probabilities or on a given rank number) can be then assigned to each song.

Based on the hypotheses enumerated above, we also experiment with three types of input features for the classifier: (1) tags; (2) words from lyrics; or (3) tags *and* lyrics. Depending on the type of features used to train the classifier and on the type of class that the classifier will assign to songs, we propose 6 experimental settings (2 types of output classes – moods and themes – and 3 types of features – tags, lyrics, tags+lyrics).

Algorithm 4.3.1 presents the main steps of our approach. We show the algorithm for mood recommendations based on tag features, the other algorithms being corresponding variants.

Algorithm 4.3.1: Tag-based Mood recommendation

1: Apply clustering method on mood classes (*optional*)
2: Select classes of moods M to be learned
2a: For each mood class
2b: If the class does not contain at least 30 songs
                     Discard class

---

[5]http://www.cs.waikato.ac.nz/~ml/weka

3: Split song set S_{total} into
   S_{train} = songs used for training the classifier
   S_{test} = songs used for testing recommendations
4: Select tag features for training the classifier
4a: For each song $s_i \in S_{train}$
4b: Create feature vector $F(s_i) = \{t_j | t_j \in T\}$,
      where
      T = set of tags from all songs in all classes
      $$t_j = \begin{cases} log(freq(t_j) + 1), \text{if } s_i \text{ has tag } t_j; \\ 0, \text{otherwise}. \end{cases}$$
5: Train Naïve Bayes classifier on S_{train}
   using $\{F(s_i); s_i \in S_{train}\}$
6: For each song $s_i \in S_{test}$
6a: Compute probability distribution $P(s_i)$ as
      $P(s_i) = \{p(m_j|s_i); m_j \in M\}$
6b: Select top k moods M_{top-k} from M
      based on $p(m_j|s_i)$
6c: Recommend M_{top-k} to the user

Step 1 of the algorithm above aims at reducing the number of mood classes to be predicted for the songs, since the 178 *AllMusic.com* mood labels are hardly distinguishable for a non-expert. This step is optional, as we experiment with all classes of moods / themes from *AllMusic.com*, as well as with a subset resulting by applying a clustering method on the original set. We present only the results for the best performing classifiers, i.e. themes clustered based on synonymy relationships (WordNet[6]) and moods clustered into primary and secondary human basic emotions [SSKO87]. The details for these clustering methods are provided at the end of this subsection.

As we need a certain amount of input data in order to be able to consistently train the classifiers, we discard those classes that have less than 30 songs assigned (step 2). After selecting separate sets of songs for training and testing in step 3 (e.g. for every fold in a 10-fold cross-validation), we build the feature vectors corresponding to each song in the training set (step 4). In the case of features based on tags, the vectors have as many elements as the total number of distinct tags assigned to the songs belonging to the mood classes. The elements of a vector will have values depending on the frequency of the tags occurring along with the song. In computing the vector elements, we experimented with different variations and automatic feature selection (e.g. Information Gain), but the formula based on the logarithm of the tag frequency provided best results and the full set of features was better suited for learning, even though it contained some noise. Once the feature vectors are constructed, they are fed into the classifier and used for training (step 5). A model is learned and afterwards is

---

[6]http://wordnet.princeton.edu

4.3 Knowledge Discovery Through Tags

applied to any new, unseen data. We can choose how many moods are recommended to the user based on the probabilities resulting from the classification or by setting an absolute threshold (steps 6a-c).

Clustering. The WordNet-based clustering of themes aims at clustering semantically related theme labels. On average, the 73 themes have 1.6 words (including stopwords; and 1.55 when discarding the stopwords). For each of the 73 themes we first process the corresponding words this theme consists of. All stop words are removed, and for the remaining words we extract the corresponding WordNet synonyms. All resulting synsets are compared pairwise and if the overlap between two sets is at least two words, the corresponding themes are clustered. With this procedure, the resulting set of themes contained 58 entries.

For manually grouping the 178 *AllMusic.com* moods we made use of the extensive work already done on studying human emotions. Though there is little agreement on the exact number of basic emotions let alone on a taxonomy including combinations of the basic concepts into complex, secondary emotions, we found the hierarchy reported in Shaver et al. [SSKO87] useful for our task (see Table 4.2). Moods are usually considered very similar to emotions but being longer in duration, less intensive and missing object directedness. For categorizing the *AllMusic.com* moods we had to slightly adapt the taxonomy to fit our data: *Surprise* was removed since no example moods were found; the same happened for some secondary emotions. Since some moods do not actually denote a mood (e.g. "literate"), we introduced a new class (*Neutral*) with three second level classes. In total, we obtained 23 second level classes ("Man. 2nd") falling into six first level classes ("Man. 1st"). We also adopted a procedure similar to the one used in [SSKO87] to build the aforementioned taxonomy of basic and secondary emotions. In a similarity sorting task, all *AllMusic.com* theme terms written on cards were sorted by the authors into as many and as high piles as seemed appropriate. Individual co-occurrence matrices were built and added to find good groupings by analyzing the clusters. Unclear membership of singular labels was resolved after discussion.

Evaluation

To measure the quality of our algorithms, we evaluate our mood and theme tag predictions against the corresponding assignments in the *AllMusic.com* dataset. Being manually created by music experts, the assignments of songs to classes of moods and themes can be considered correct and thus accepted as ground truth. Since our goal is recommendation of relevant annotations, we perform a standard 10-fold cross-validation and evaluate our results choosing the standard following IR metrics: Hit rate at rank k ($H@k$), R-Precision (RP) and Mean Reciprocal Rank (MRR). We concentrate on the $H@3$ metric, as we recommend three annotations to the users to choose from. We consider three annotations a good compromise, between providing enough suggestions and at the same time not overwhelming the users with too much

Primary (Man. 1st)	Secondary Emotion (Man. 2nd)
Love	Affection, Lust, Longing
Joy	Cheerfulness, Zest, Pride, Optimism, Contentment, Enthrallment, Relief
Surprise	Surprise
Anger	Irritation, Exasperation, Rage, Disgust, Envy, Torment
Sadness	Suffering, Sadness, Disappointment, Shame, Neglect, Sympathy
Fear	Horror, Nervousness

Table 4.2 Hierarchy of basic human emotions [SSKO87]

	Clustering	Classes	Features	H@3	H@5	RP	MRR
Themes	-	11	Random	0.29	0.47	0.10	0.28
	-	11	Tags	0.80	0.92	0.49	0.67
	-	11	Lyrics	0.56*	0.72*	0.26*	0.46*
	-	11	Tags+Lyrics	0.80*+	0.94+	0.48*+	0.67*+
	WordNet	9	Random	0.36	0.58	0.12	0.33
	WordNet	9	Tags	0.85	0.94	0.47	0.66
	WordNet	9	Lyrics	0.72*	0.85*	0.38*	0.59*
	WordNet	**9**	**Tags+Lyrics**	**0.88+**	**0.96+**	**0.48+**	**0.69+**
Moods	-	89	Random	0.06	0.09	0.02	0.08
	-	89	Tags	0.39	0.51	0.17	0.34
	-	89	Lyrics	0.17*	0.25*	0.06*	0.17*
	-	89	Tags+Lyrics	0.37+	0.48+	0.15+	0.32+
	Man. 1st	6	Random	0.61	0.89	0.23	0.47
	Man. 1st	6	Tags	0.88	0.99	0.49	0.71
	Man. 1st	6	Lyrics	0.82*	0.98	0.42*	0.65*
	Man. 1st	**6**	**Tags+Lyrics**	**0.89*+**	**0.99**	**0.52+**	**0.73+**
	Man. 2nd	22	Random	0.21	0.33	0.07	0.22
	Man. 2nd	22	Tags	0.63	0.76	0.31	0.53
	Man. 2nd	22	Lyrics	0.49*	0.65*	0.21*	0.41*
	Man. 2nd	**22**	**Tags+Lyrics**	**0.64+**	**0.78+**	**0.31+**	**0.52+**

Table 4.3 Experimental results: $H@3$, $H@5$, RP, MRR for the different algorithms along with a random baseline for comparison. A $*$ or a $+$ states a statistically significant difference (one-tail paired t-Test with $p < 0.05$) with respect to tags or lyrics as features, respectively (per clustering method).

information. We present the results for all our experimental runs in Table 4.3.

4.3 Knowledge Discovery Through Tags 87

We observe that the best performing methods are those using tags as input features for the classifiers. The methods using only lyrics as features perform worst. When combining tags and lyrics as features, the corresponding methods perform much better than those based only on lyrics and they sometimes also slightly outperform the tag-based methods. These results confirm once more the quality of user provided tags, as well as hypothesis 1 on which our approach relies (see Section 4.3.2). Lyrics, in contrast to tags, introduce noise, as many song texts contain all sorts of interjections (e.g. "hey", "uh-huh", etc.), slang or simply informal English. With lyrics features the best results are obtained for genre and theme recommendations. This related to the second hypothesis on which we built our approach. Though alone they are obviously not descriptive enough to decide well upon theme, by setting the topic, lyrics seem to help removing some tag ambiguity, thus enabling identifying appropriate themes. In contrast, lyrics do not seem to be indicative of the mood of a song.

For the case of theme recommendations, the best results, $H@3$ of 0.88, are achieved for the algorithm using a combination of tags and lyrics as features and applying a WordNet synonymy based clustering on the theme classes. Compared to themes, mood recommendations do not perform as well when using many classes, achieving only a $H@3$ of 0.64. For the case of moods, we present the results corresponding to both first and second level manual clustering of the original *AllMusic.com* classes (rows "Man. 1st" and "Man. 2nd"). Reducing the cluster number to the 6 first level classes ("Man. 1st") corresponding roughly to basic human emotions, boosts the performance considerably and for the best method using tags and lyrics as input features we achieve a $H@3$ value of 0.89. Though having a larger mood vocabulary for recommendations should be aimed at, trade-offs are necessary. It is an interesting question for future work, how many classes are appropriate to describe what mood distinctions people actually do when listening or referring to music.

Micro-evaluating results moreover per specific annotation class, shows that while some classes are relatively easy to recommend, others may require special attention or some level of disambiguation. Table 4.4 shows $H@3$ values for the different classes without applying any clustering method and using tags as features. In general, classes which are hard to recommend are ambiguous and the annotations are mostly subjective. Themes like "Late Night" or "Summertime" strongly depend on the person and what s/he is used to be doing late night or in summer. The same is true for moods like "Precious" or "Rambunctious", as they can be subjectively interpreted in several ways. On the other hand, classes which can be recommended with high accuracy are also more clearly defined, may it be a theme like "Slow Dance" or a mood like "Hypnotic". Interestingly, for neither moods nor themes we found a correlation between the a priori probability of a class, i.e. its size in terms of positive examples in the dataset, and performance.

We also evaluated the quality of our recommended themes for music tracks in terms of user judgments. Thus, we set up a user survey as a Facebook application[7]

---
[7]For details on the survey and application, please refer to [BFNP08] or access http://www.

	Best	#Docs	H@3	Worst	#Docs	H@3
Themes	Slow Dance	40	0.97	Late Night	26	0.52
	Romantic Evening	27	0.89	Summertime	43	0.62
	Autumn	36	0.89	Party Time	29	0.72
Moods	Ethereal	40	0.65	Precious	33	0.00
	Hypnotic	47	0.64	Calm/Peaceful	33	0.00
	Angst-Ridden	61	0.57	Rambunctious	30	0.00

Table 4.4 Examples of best and worst performing (by $H@3$) classes, without clustering, learned using tags as features. #Docs gives the number of music tracks used in the experiments per mood/theme.

(see Figure 4.3), where users had to manually label songs with one or more theme classes used in our algorithms and in *AllMusic.com*.

With this user survey, we aimed to compare not only the performance of normal users against the *AllMusic.com* experts, but also the results of our algorithm against the choices of the users.

The results show that our method performs well also with respect to the user assignments. The fact that the users perform quite bad compared to the *AllMusic.com* experts, but our method performs well both compared to the users and to the experts, indicates that our method provides theme labels that are easier to recognize by users than the labels assigned by AllMusic experts and thus helps for bridging the gap between the users' and music experts' vocabularies.

4.3.3 Deriving Moods for Pictures

Similar to the case of music, our analysis for pictures showed some clear gap between the tagging and the querying vocabulary. Here, a large portion of tags refer to location information, such as the country or city where the picture has been taken. However, queries targeting images much more often name subjective aspects of the objects or persons depicted on the photos, e.g. "scary", "rage" or "funny". In this section we will present an approach which aims at bridging exactly this gap.

Picture Mood Recommendation Algorithm

Recommendations of mood annotations in case of pictures, rely only on tag information. Unlike for music, where we could also exploit the lyrics of the songs, for *Flickr* pictures, the only available textual information comes from tag data[8]. The

---
facebook.com/apps/application.php?id=20699508679

[8]Other types of textual metadata, like titles, descriptions, comments, group memberships, etc., could have been also used, but we wanted to keep this approach generalizable to other photo sharing

4.3 Knowledge Discovery Through Tags

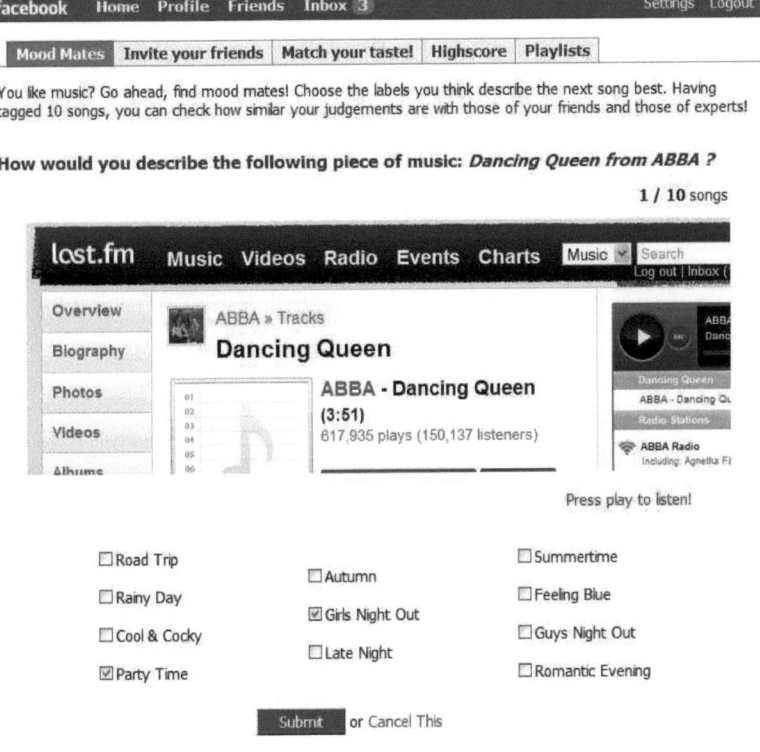

Figure 4.3 Mood Mates! Facebook application

assumption on which we base our recommendation is similar to the case of pictures, namely that the existing tags attached to photos can possibly provide information regarding the corresponding mood of the pictures.

Given the crawling methodology which was used for pictures and in order to ensure a fair classification of the data, all tags related to a mood or emotion were deleted. To this end, we looked up in WordNet all the labels included in our emotion taxonomy and collected all corresponding word forms of the most popular sense including synonyms, as well as all their derivationally related forms. The resulting list of terms was used to remove all matching tags of the collected *Flickr* pictures (dataset **F**, described in Section 4.3.1). This approach has been inspired from works focusing

---

systems, as well.

on personalization methods, where for evaluation parts of the users preferences are removed in order to be later inferred by the proposed personalization algorithms (see [CLWB00, CZG+09]).

The remaining tags are used as input features for training a multi-class classifier over all classes of moods. Like in the case of music, here we also make use of the Weka implementation for the Naïve Bayes Multinomial classifier, which produces for all pictures in the test set probability distributions over all classes of moods.

Evaluation

Like for music mood and theme recommendations, for pictures we also aim at evaluating the quality of the recommended mood labels. As ground truth data we use the data collected from *Flickr* (set **F**), since all these pictures have been manually assigned by users to *Flickr* groups centered around human emotions/moods. All pictures pertaining to a specific mood class represent the positive training examples, while pictures taken randomly from the rest of the classes build up the set of negative examples. In all cases the number of positive and negative examples for a class is equally balanced.

A first set of experiments aimed at recommending mood labels corresponding to the primary human emotions and in this case, the classes to be learned by the classifiers consisted of the union of all data belonging to all underlying secondary emotions (e.g. the Love class comprises all data gathered from the *Flickr* groups for Affection, Lust and Longing). Similarly, another experimental run focused on secondary emotion label recommendations, and in this case each secondary emotion class represented a class to be learned. We perform 10-fold cross validation and evaluate the performance of our method according to the same set of IR metrics, which was used also for music: Hit rate at rank k ($H@k$), R-Precision (RP) and Mean Reciprocal Rank (MRR). All results are summarized in Table 4.5.

The results confirm once more the hypothesis on which we based our recommendation approach: existing tags can give good indications regarding the corresponding moods of the pictures. All recommendations corresponding to the primary human emotions achieved very high quality, with a value close to 1 for $H@3$ and even a $H@1$ between 0.71 and 0.91. We also compute the overall performance over all primary emotion classes, as averages weighted by the number of instances corresponding to each class. The results are very good, with a 0.97 value for $H@3$ and 0.93 for MRR.

Only for "Surprise" the results were somewhat poorer, with $H@1$ of 0.61 and MRR of 0.77. This situation may arise due to the fact that the only *Flickr* group which we could select for this mood, was less focused (named "Shocking, Surprise and General Wide Eyes!!"). Looking in detail at the confusion matrix (Figure 4.4A), this becomes visible: "Surprise" is often misclassified as "Fear". A clear distinction seems to be difficult for our *Flickr* users. The same fact was also indicated by psychological studies which reported that fear and surprise expressions are easily differentiated

4.3 Knowledge Discovery Through Tags

	Mood	#Docs	H@1	H@3	H@5	RP	MRR
Primary Emotions	*[Random]*	–	*0.17*	*0.50*	*0.83*	*0.17*	*0.41*
	[Overall]	**52,426**	**0.89**	**0.97**	**0.99**	**0.89**	**0.93**
	Fear	7,248	0.87	0.99	1	0.87	0.93
	Sadness	40,602	0.91	0.96	0.99	0.91	0.94
	Joy	1,062	0.77	0.95	1	0.77	0.86
	Love	1,184	0.71	0.94	0.99	0.7	0.83
	Anger	1,695	0.84	0.94	0.99	0.84	0.89
	Surprise	635	0.61	0.93	0.98	0.61	0.77
Secondary Emotions	*[Random]*	–	*0.06*	*0.18*	*0.29*	*0.06*	*0.20*
	[Overall]	**52,452**	**0.89**	**0.97**	**0.98**	**0.89**	**0.93**
	Horror	6,881	0.84	0.98	0.99	0.84	0.91
	Neglect	36,943	0.94	0.98	0.99	0.94	0.96
	Sadness	3,684	0.73	0.98	0.99	0.73	0.85
	Nervousness	367	0.95	0.96	0.98	0.95	0.96
	Torment	823	0.88	0.96	0.97	0.88	0.92
	Rage	680	0.92	0.95	0.99	0.92	0.94
	Cheerfulness	443	0.88	0.93	0.95	0.88	0.92
	Surprise	635	0.59	0.91	0.97	0.59	0.75
	Longing	1,011	0.7	0.89	0.98	0.69	0.81
	Relief	78	0.54	0.74	0.87	0.54	0.67
	Disgust	98	0.53	0.63	0.71	0.53	0.63
	Pride	112	0.44	0.63	0.79	0.44	0.58
	Optimism	308	0.46	0.61	0.81	0.46	0.6
	Affection	124	0.26	0.52	0.73	0.26	0.46
	Zest	122	0.18	0.39	0.58	0.18	0.37
	Irritation	94	0.17	0.28	0.35	0.17	0.31
	Lust	49	0.06	0.18	0.47	0.06	0.25

Table 4.5 Experimental results: $H@1$, $H@3$, $H@5$, RP, MRR for the different algorithms over all picture moods, i.e. primary and secondary emotions; #Docs gives the number of pictures per emotion. [Overall] shows the weighted average by the number of instances in the mood class; [Random] is the random baseline for comparison.

from other basic emotions, but are often confused with each other both in labeling and posing facial expressions [EO79].

For primary emotions, correlation between class size and performance is medium: Pearson's r is 0.45 for $H@3$ and 0.63 for $H@1$, RP, and MRR. Thus, when misclassifying instances the classifier is biased to incorrectly assigning one of the two dominant classes "Fear" or "Sadness". Besides, these two emotions are very close together in the cluster analysis of the mood label space of [SSKO87][9]. Both share the same nega-

---
[9] Participants had to sort emotion labels into piles of related emotions, thus establishing a hier-

A) Primary Emotions

		\multicolumn{6}{c}{Predicted Class}					
		a	b	c	d	e	f
Correct Class	a = Anger	1438	96	21	32	96	12
	b = Sadness	316	37004	630	334	1878	440
	c = Love	10	100	882	36	101	55
	d = Joy	8	102	25	817	66	44
	e = Fear	58	643	63	55	6337	92
	f = Surprise	5	21	11	41	172	385

B) Secondary Emotions

		a	b	c	d	e	f	g	h	i	j	k	l	m	n	o	p	q
	a = Longing	720		171			11	49	32	1		10	1		1		15	
	b = Pride	1	54	16				7	9	1		7	1		2		14	
	c = Sadness	82		2708			30	346	442	1	3	13	4		19		36	
	d = Lust	2		9	2				29			1					6	
	e = Relief			2		44	1	2	12	1		3					13	
	f = Rage	5		6			626	16	25					1	1			
	g = Neglect	158	17	665	2	5	66	35031	607	14	13	71	33	41	136	3	59	22
Correct Class	h = Horror	28		400			27	493	5801	1	6	23	2	2	26	2	69	1
	i = Affection	1		24				2	19	37		4			1		36	
	j = Nervousness			9					5		350	1					2	
	k = Cheerfulness	3	1	8		1	5	11				394	2		1		17	
	l = Optimism	9		36		2	43	35	2			11	143		3		24	
	m = Zest	9		12			1	50	15			7		23			4	
	n = Torment	4		24			1	23	26			2			740		3	
	o = Disgust			1				7	33	1		1	2			52	1	
	p = Surprise	5		54			1	11	176	1	3	9	2	2	2		369	
	q = Irritation	5		18			1	24	20			5	1				5	15

Figure 4.4 Confusion matrices for A) primary and B) secondary emotions as image moods

tive valence but with different intensity. However, fear may range from low intensity (i.e. being worried) to very high intensity (i.e. being panicked). Investigating the tag features used in learning these classes, similar tags are ranked highly according to their information gain, though all tags have rather small values in general.

The overall weighted results for the secondary human emotion label recommendations are almost identical with the case of primary emotions. If the averages are not weighted by class prevalence, the overall unweighted averages for secondary emotions are about 0.2 lower compared to their counterparts for primary emotions. This is due to the weighting process favoring the overly frequent and well predicted classes "Neglect" and "Sadness" (corresponding to the primary emotion "Sadness") and "Horror" (with "Fear" as primary emotion). As "Sadness" and "Fear" examples are also highly prominent in our experiment for primary emotions, the overall results reported in Table 4.5 are similar. In general, correlation between *a priori* probability of a class and performance is smaller for secondary emotions: Pearson's r is between 0.32 and 0.37 for the different evaluation measures. As a result, "Neglect", "Horror" and

---

archy/clusters of basic and secondary emotions

"Sadness" are predicted wrongly more often then the remaining classes. Still, the confusion matrix from Figure 4.4B indicates some interesting patterns not only explainable by classifier bias. "Longing" is very often misclassified as "Sadness", much more than as the top frequent "Neglect" or "Horror". Although both belong to different primary emotions ("Love" vs. "Sadness") and are rather far apart in the cluster analysis of emotion labels, for *Flickr* users they seem to share the negative valence and low arousal. Again, "Surprise" gets easily confused with the fear related emotion of "Horror".

When inspecting the results over the different mood classes, we can see that for some classes, e.g., "Affection", "Zest", "Irritation" and "Lust", performance is considerably lower with $H@3$ ranging from 0.18 to 0.52. The main reason for these results is the relatively small number of pictures contained in each of these groups, which implicitly made learning more difficult. Moreover, manually inspecting the corresponding group of *Flickr* photos for all those four classes, we found it difficult to identify pictures depicting only the intended state of mind for each particular *Flickr* group. For example, we could observe a large number of "Affection" pictures depicting sad/crying people and implicitly a large amount of tags close to the set of tags belonging to the "Sadness" class. Given the relatively small set of pictures, the influence of such 'ambiguous' photos and implicitly their associated set of tags becomes critical.

For all other mood classes, we achieve $H@3$ values over 0.6, for about half of the classes even 0.90 and more, the best results being obtained for the class "Neglect" – 0.98 for $H@3$ and 0.96 for MRR.

Having used the same measures as in the case of music mood and theme recommendations, we can directly compare the two sets of results. In Figure 4.5 we depict the $H@3$ and MRR values for all best performing theme and mood recommendation algorithms for music and pictures.

For music, both theme and primary mood label recommendations achieve almost equal $H@3$ values of 0.88. Recommendations from the secondary mood classes are more error prone, achieving only 0.64 $H@3$. For the case of pictures, we do not observe any difference for either primary or secondary mood recommendations. Moreover, recommendations for picture resources are of higher quality, probably due to the data which was used as ground truth: mood-related *Flickr* groups, manually created by users. The ground truth gathered from *AllMusic.com*, given the extremely high number of mood classes and implicit redundancy, had to be mapped to the hierarchy of human emotions. This process potentially introduces some noise into the data.

4.4 Event Detection from Tags

With the rapidly increasing popularity of Social Media sites, a lot of user generated content has been injected in the Web, resulting in a large amount of both multimedia

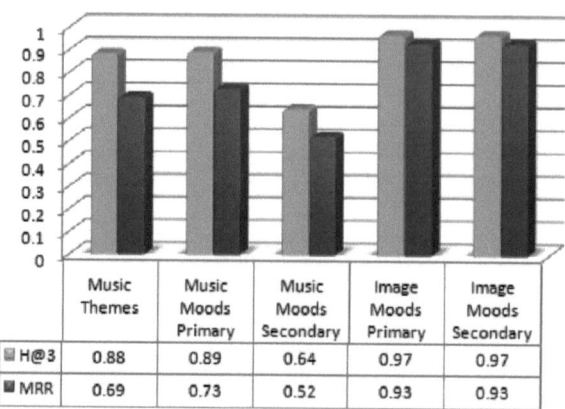

Figure 4.5 $H@3$ and MRR values across our best music, image, mood and theme recommendations

items (music – *Last.fm*, *MySpace*, pictures – *Flickr*, *Picasa*, videos – *YouTube*) and textual data (tags and other text-based documents). As a consequence, it has become more and more difficult using standard IR techniques to find exactly the content that matches the users' information needs. Organizing different media types together with textual content in the form of events became an emerging presentation model and tries to alleviate this problem. The methods we propose in this section focus on the domain of pictures, in particular on a subset of *Flickr* data. Many of the photos posted by users on Flickr have been shot during events and our methods aim to allow browsing or organization of picture collections in a natural way, by events. The algorithms we introduce in this section exploit the tags provided by users, for classifying pictures into different event categories. The extensive automated experiments demonstrate that our approach is very effective and opens new possibilities for multimedia retrieval, in particular image search.

4.4.1 Data Set Descriptions

For the purpose of our experiments we had to collect an extensive set of *Flickr* pictures, and more importantly, ground truth data. Identifying a good ground truth set for events (in particular for pictures) turned out to be quite difficult. The main reason for this is the lack of a verified and largely accepted event taxonomy (ontology). One of the most known events categorization is the Yahoo! Upcoming events

4.4 Event Detection from Tags

catalog, however it's thirteen categories are not extensive enough. Using WordNet[10] was also not an option in our case, as *Flickr* tags can be written in many different ways (intentionally or unintentionally) by the users and thus not matchable with the WordNet database. Wikipedia[11] has also its' own event taxonomy[12], but here the categorization is not easily understandable. Besides, several possibilities are listed regarding to how to organize events (e.g. by location, topic, year, etc.), and these different categorizations introduce ambiguities, as they are not mutually exclusive and do not cover all possible facets of a good event classification.

To cope with this problem, we decided to make use of the YAGO ontology, which brings together WordNet and Wikipedia knowledge. In the following we present its' most important features and characteristics.

The YAGO Ontology

YAGO[SKW07][13] is a large and extensible ontology that builds on entities and relations from Wikipedia. Facts in YAGO have been automatically extracted from Wikipedia and unified with semantics from WordNet, achieving an accuracy of around 95%. All objects (e.g., cities, people, even URLs) are represented as entities in the YAGO model. The hierarchy of classes starts with the Wikipedia categories containing a page and relies on WordNet's well-defined taxonomy of homonyms to establish further *subClassOf* relations. We make use of these *subClassOf* relations in YAGO, which provide us with semantic concepts describing Wikipedia entities. We also rely on the *type* relation, deducting what higher level concept a page is about.

Events Collection

For collecting event names, we thus made use of the YAGO ontology and selected only those entities having a *type* (YAGO relation) *wordnet_event*. With this method we retrieved a list of 138,794 Wikipedia event page titles, like "Reichstag fire", "Battle of the Nile", "CeBIT", or "Iranian presidential election, 2009". We will refer to this list of events as [*events*] later in our experiments. Starting from [*events*] we retrieved the Wikipedia categories assigned to the Wikipedia pages, i.e. to the events, using the *subClassOf* relation in YAGO. Thus we have a total of 25,223 distinct Wikipedia categories assigned to [*events*] – later called [*categories*]. Furthermore, we also retrieved the WordNet concepts of [*categories*] using again *subClassOf* relations starting from [*categories*]. This set of 1,521 distinct WordNet concepts will be referred as [*concepts*]. Thus we have an extensive list of [*events*], along with the corresponding [*categories*] and the super-[*concepts*], forming a three-level hierarchical taxonomy.

---

[10] http://wordnet.princeton.edu/
[11] http://en.wikipedia.org/wiki/Main_Page
[12] http://en.wikipedia.org/wiki/Category:Events
[13] Available for download at http://www.mpi-inf.mpg.de/yago-naga/yago/downloads.html

Flickr Images

Having now an extensive set of event categories, the next step corresponded to gathering the actual ground truth data, consisting of *Flickr* images. For this purpose we made use of the *Flickr* API[14]. We started from the 138,794 Wikipedia event pages and crawled the corresponding *Flickr* groups. Being explicitly created by users and containing pictures contributed by a multitude of users, these *Flickr* groups quite accurately represent social groups interested in the specific events and represent thus a good ground truth. For gathering the *Flickr* groups we made use of the '*flickr.groups.search*' method and kept the first hit in the results list. With this method we could gather 29,796 event-related *Flickr* groups.

In the next step, for all retrieved groups, we collected their corresponding group pools, i.e. all pictures contributed by all users to the corresponding groups. In total the number of pictures gathered was 13,310,523 and among them 11,125,422 unique pictures.

Finally, for all collected photos, we needed the tag information, i.e. raw and normalized form of the attached tags, as well as the Id and name of the user assigning the tag. 1,830,053 tags have been gathered with this method (187,934 unique ones).

4.4.2 Event Detection Methods

For classifying images into the different categories of events we base our solution on collaboratively created social knowledge, i.e. tags associated with *Flickr* pictures. Based on already provided user tags, we build classifiers which try to assign the pictures to the corresponding event categories. More specifically, our approach relies on the hypothesis, that the existing tags provided by users for a particular photo carry information which can be used to infer the event category this picture belongs to. We perform a preprocessing step on the data collected from *Flickr* and we also experiment with different types of clustering methods on the original datasets. Below we describe the details of our algorithm, together with the preprocessing and photo clustering steps.

Clustering of Flickr Pictures

In the approach we propose, we experimented with different ways of organizing the pictures crawled from *Flickr*. Besides the original, unclustered dataset, two additional types of hierarchical clustering are considered, based on Wikipedia and WordNet classes, respectively. Below we present the details:

Original dataset (Unclustered). As described in Sections 4.4.1, 4.4.1 and 4.4.1, we start collecting the pictures by considering the YAGO entities having as type

---
[14] http://www.flickr.com/services/api/

4.4 Event Detection from Tags   97

Nr.	Flickr Group	Event	Wiki class	WordNet class
1	24165441@N00	intl_day_of_peace	unit_nat_day	day
2	602639@N25	intl_holocaust_rembr_day	unit_nat_day	day
3	1172355@N23	motorama	auto_shows	show
4	84783197@N00	australian_intl_motor_show	auto_shows	attraction

Table 4.6 Example for clustering Flickr pictures

wordnet_event and their corresponding Wikipedia event pages. The *Flickr* groups we can identify as first hits in response to queries consisting of the Wikipedia event page's name correspond then to the list of [*events*]. For the example in Table 4.6, the list [*events*] consists of all entries in column '*Event*' and the pictures collected for the corresponding *Flickr* groups identified for these events remain unclustered.

Clustering based on Wikipedia classes. The first method of clustering we applied relies on the Wikipedia classes. In this case, all pictures belonging to the *Flickr* groups having the same Wikipedia class are merged into one cluster. The list of [*categories*] thus contains all unique entries from the column '*Wiki_class*', i.e. *united_nations_day* and *auto_shows* (for the example in Table 4.6). The pictures corresponding to the group Ids in rows 1 and 2 will be merged and the resulting cluster corresponds to the
united_nations_day 'category'. Similarly, pictures corresponding to the groups from rows 3 and 4 will be put together.

Clustering based on WordNet classes. The second type of clustering we employed made use of the WordNet classes. For this case, similar to clustering based on Wikipedia classes, all pictures belonging to the *Flickr* groups having the same WordNet class are merged into one cluster. Rows 1 and 2 from Table 4.6 will be merged and will correspond to the *day* WordNet class. Rows 3 and 4 will remain untouched, as their WordNet classes are different. For this particular example, the list of [*concepts*] will be composed of *day*, *show* and *attraction*.

The photo event detection algorithm is then run on all these three variations of our dataset, i.e. clustered or unclustered.

Event Detection Algorithm

The core of our photo event detection algorithm is a probabilistic classifier trained on the *Flickr* ground truth using tags as input features. Separate classifiers correspond to the different types of event classes that we extracted from YAGO. For building the classifiers, we use the open source machine learning library Weka[15]. In the experiments presented, we use the Naïve Bayes Multinomial implementation available

---

[15] http://www.cs.waikato.ac.nz/~ml/weka

in Weka. We also experimented with other classifiers (e.g. Support Vector Machines, Decision Trees), which resulted in similar classification performances, but were much more computationally intensive. Moreover, we also experimented with feature selection based on automatic methods (e.g. Information Gain) but the results showed that the full set is better suitable for learning, even though it contains some noise.

We have one classifier for each event category that we aim to learn to classify. The positive examples are represented by the pictures gathered from the event's corresponding *Flickr* group / resulted cluster, while the negative ones are randomly selected from the pictures corresponding to the rest of the event classes. The number of positive and negative examples is almost equally balanced. This classifier produces for every photo in the test set an output, such as 1 – i.e. the photo belongs to this type of event, or 0 – i.e. the photo can belong to any other event category, but this one.

Algorithm 4.4.1 presents the main steps of our approach.

Algorithm 4.4.1: Event detection

1: **Cluster *Flickr* pictures** (*optional*, see Section 4.4.2)
2: **Data preprocessing** step (see Section 4.4.2)
3: **For each** *event / category / concept*, E_x
4:   **Split picture collection**, P_{total} into
5: P_{train} = pictures used for training the classifier
6: P_{test} = pictures used for testing the classifier
7:   **Select tag features** for training the classifier
8:   **For each** photo $p_i \in P_{train}$
9:   **Create feature vector** $F(p_i) = \{t_j | t_j \in T\}$,
10: T = set of tags from all photos
11: $t_j = \begin{cases} 1, P_i \text{ has tag } t_j; \\ 0, \text{otherwise.} \end{cases}$
12:   **Train Naïve Bayes** classifier on P_{train}
        using $\{F(p_i); p_i \in P_{train}\}$
13:   **For each** photo $p_i \in P_{test}$
14:   **Compute** classifier **output**, $NB(p_i)$
15:   If $(NB(p_i) == 1)$ classify p_i in E_x

Step 1 of the algorithm above aims at reducing the number of event classes to be predicted for the photos. This step is optional (described in detail in Section 4.4.2), as we experiment with all classes of events extracted from YAGO, as well as with a subset resulted from applying one of the clustering methods on the original set. If two or more classes are clustered based on one the methods described in Section 4.4.2, the resulted class will contain all pictures which have been originally assigned to the

4.4 Event Detection from Tags

composing classes. As we need a certain amount of input data in order to be able to consistently train the classifiers, we discard those classes containing less than 100 photos (step 2) and the details of this pruning step are described in Section 4.4.2.

After selecting separate sets of pictures for training and testing (steps 4 - 6), we build the feature vectors corresponding to each picture in the training set (lines 7 - 11). The vectors have as many elements as the total number of distinct tags assigned to the images belonging to the event / category / concept classes. The elements of a vector will have values of either 1 or 0, depending on whether the tag has been assigned to the particular photo, or not. Once the feature vectors are constructed, they are fed into the classifier and used for training (step 12). A model is learned and afterwards is applied to any new, unseen data. For the unseen picture, if the output of the classifier is 1, the picture will be assigned to the current class.

Data Preprocessing

Since for training the event classifiers we need enough data at our disposal, we need to perform a preprocessing step and remove those groups / group clusters not having sufficient photo instances. The preprocessing actions' flow looks as follows:

Algorithm 4.4.2: Data proprocessing

1: **For each** *event/category/concept* class
2:     **Repeat until** nothing to discard anymore
3:         **Discard tags** corresponding to:
4:             - names of Wikipedia event pages
5:             - words composing event names
6:             - synonyms of words composing event names
7:             - combinations of words / synonyms
8:         **Discard tags**, t_i, where $freq(t_i) < 10$
9:             over all *event/category/concept* classes
10:        **Discard photos** p_i, where $nrTags(p_i) \notin [2, 75]$
11:        **Discard class**, c_i of *event/category/concept* if
12:             $nrPhotos(c_i) < 100$

As we can see in lines 3 through 7, all tags appearing in the name of the Wikipedia event page, together with their combinations and synonyms are removed from the pictures in the collection corresponding to the specific *Flickr* group (or resulted cluster, as described in Section 4.4.2). With this step we avoid the potential bias of the classifiers towards words which might indicate the appartenance of the photos to the corresponding classes of events / categories / concepts.

Tags which do not appear together with at least 10 photos throughout the collection are discarded (lines 8, 9), as they might represent too obscure annotations, or even misspellings – and thus do not have any positive influence on the classification, or might even introduce noise. Similarly, photos with less than 2 tags are removed from the collection, as well as photos having more than 75 tags, since they might contain spam-tags [KEG+07] (line 10). Finally, the classes of events / categories / concepts with less than 100 photos are also removed (lines 11 and 12), since we need sufficient instances in order to be able to train the classifiers. The whole process is repeated until no more pruning can be made.

4.4.3 Evaluation

Experimental Setup

As already described in Section 4.4.2, we experiment with three different datasets:

- We aim to classify the events themselves and we create separate classifiers for all [*events*], with data coming from *Flickr* groups we can identify the YAGO events and their corresponding Wikipedia event pages. Below we will refer to the results for this dataset as *YagoGroups*.

- We also experiment with classifying the Wikipedia categories, containing the events. As described in Section 4.4.2, *Flickr* groups get clustered based on their common Wikipedia categories. In this case, we build classifiers for all [*categories*] and we will refer to this set of results as *YagoWikiCats*.

- Finally, we aim to classify the WordNet concepts describing the Wikipedia categories, i.e. some higher level event-centered concepts. For this, we build classifiers for all [*concepts*], which we feed with data resulted from aggregating the *Flickr* group pools having the same WordNet class. In the results section below, this will be referred to as *YagoWordnet*.

With this evaluation we focus on automatically measuring the quality of the photo event classification algorithm. As ground truth data we use the information collected from the *Flickr* photo groups, or the resulted clustered sets. Being manually created by humans, the assignments of photos to the different classes of events can be considered correct and thus accepted as ground truth. Besides, through the collaborative participation of more users to the groups, i.e. by both joining the emerging networks and by contributing content in terms of pictures, comments, tags, etc., we can ensure that the spam-groups will be filtered out[16].

---

[16]Like in the case of tagging, correct and suitable tags will get more and more employed, while obscure / misspelled tags will be pushed to the tail of the power law frequency distribution [GH06, HRS07].

4.4 Event Detection from Tags

	# Classif.	Avg. Inst.	# Feat.
YagoGroups	357	622.68	14,366
YagoWikiCats	96	683.95	5,735
YagoWordnet	51	4,503.37	15,239

Table 4.7 Statistics for the three expriment sets

	Acc[%]	P[%]	R[%]
YagoGroups	80.15	75.21	91.50
YagoWikiCats	84.77	80.29	93.50
YagoWordnet	79.88	76.50	87.57

Table 4.8 Averaged classification results for the three experimental runs

For the three types of experiments, we present in Table 4.7 some statistics regarding the number of classifiers built (column '# Classif.'), average number of instances for each classifier (column 'Avg. Inst.') and the number of features, respectively ('# Feat.').

The numbers in Table 4.7 are all computed after performing the pruning step, as described in Algorithm 4.4.1 (see Section 4.4.2). As we can observe, many groups have been discarded because of not containing enough data.

For evaluating the performance of our algorithms, we inspect the classification accuracy (Acc), precision (P) and recall (R) measures, when performing 10-fold cross-validation on the datasets. In Table 4.8 we present the results of the evaluation runs and in Table 4.9 we present a set of the best and worst performing classifiers.

Results

We observe that the average classification accuracy for all three datasets is very good, almost in all cases being above 80%. Using tags as input features for the classification is thus very convenient, as tags can be easily collected along with the resources they are attached to. These results confirm once more the quality of user provided tags – a result also observed in [BFNP08] – as well as the hypothesis on which our approach relies (see Section 4.4.2).

In Figure 4.6, for a better comparison among the three experimental runs, we depict the averaged values of accuracy, precision and recall. We can observe that our method is not susceptible to the number of classes available for the classification (see column '# Classif.' in Table 4.7 and results in Table 4.8). Even if in the case of *YagoGroups*, i.e. the original, unclustered dataset, we have 357 event classes, the average accuracy is 80.15%. For *YagoWordnet*, although there are much less classes to distinguish among, the performance is a bit poorer than in the case of *YagoGroups*. The reason for these results is the fact that the WordNet event categories represent

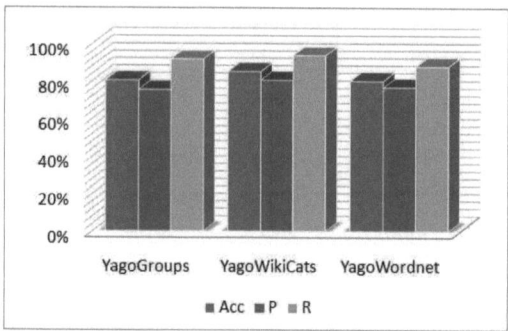

Figure 4.6 Classification results (Acc, P, R) for the three experimental runs

some more abstract event-related concepts. By clustering the initial set of *Flickr* social groups based on their common WordNet categories, the resulting sets of pictures corresponding to each of these WordNet event concepts are becoming too heterogeneous. Thus, it becomes more difficult for the classifiers to correctly distinguish among classes.

For the *YagoWikiCats* on the other hand, the performance is best among the three sets of results. In this case we also cluster the initial *Flickr* groups' pools of pictures. However, even if the resulted clusters gather also all pictures from the composing *Flickr* groups, the resulting sets are still homogeneous. This is due to the fact that the Wikipedia categories are more abstract than the YAGO events, yet the abstraction is not introducing any noise in the classification. The clustering in this case is even reducing some of the ambiguities of the *YagoGroups* sets of photos, these initial sets being perhaps a bit too fine grained.

The results presented so far (Table 4.8, Figure 4.6) indicate the performance of our algorithms in classifying photos into the different classes of [*events*], [*categories*] and [*concepts*], i.e. *macro* evaluation results. However, we were also interested in *micro*-evaluating our algorithms. More specifically, we also analyzed the results per specific event / category / concept class to find out which classes offer the best performances and which classes are more difficult to learn. Table 4.9 shows the *Acc*, *P* and *R* values, together with the available number of photo instances for training the classifiers. We selected some of the best and worst performing classifiers and the results are grouped based on the three different experimental runs.

The differences show that while some classes are relatively easy to learn, others may require special attention or some level of disambiguation. Also, classes which are hard to learn are ambiguous and the annotations are mostly subjective. As we can see, a higher number of instances available for training, definitely improves the classification accuracy: five of the nine best performing classifiers had more than

	Performance	Event/Categ./Concept Class	Acc[%]	P	R	# Inst.
YagoGroups	Best	Clare_Minor_Hurling_Championship	98.82	0.98	1.00	254
		Grand_Prix_de_Pau	98.09	0.97	0.99	680
		Colorado_Castle_Rocks	98.03	0.97	0.99	304
	Worst	Before_Sunrise	65.20	0.12	0.60	102
		A_Night_Full_of_Rain	62.61	0.19	0.59	234
		Heavy_Metal_Parking_Lot	60.29	0.01	0.56	136
YagoWikiCats	Best	wikicategory_Disney_parks_and_attractions	99.28	0.99	1.0	1,392
		wikicategory_Sports_in_Pittsburgh_Pennsylvania	97.87	0.96	0.99	1,832
		wikicategory_Auto_shows	97.00	0.94	1.00	200
	Worst	wikicategory_CBC_network_shows	74.09	0.18	0.71	440
		wikicategory_Beauty_pageants	73.24	0.13	0.68	284
		wikicategory_2008_NASCAR_Sprint_Cup_races	65.31	0.27	0.63	490
YagoWordnet	Best	wordnet_championship	93.84	0.93	0.98	326
		wordnet_park	90.30	0.84	1.00	1,392
		wordnet_battle	88.79	0.86	0.93	2,462
	Worst	wordnet_execution	70.33	0.65	0.87	364
		wordnet_motion	69.08	0.67	0.76	760
		wordnet_television_program	66.36	0.62	0.84	1,400

Table 4.9 Examples of best and worst performing (by Acc) classifiers for the different experimental runs

500 instances at their disposal. Nevertheless, for very clear event categories, like *wikicategory_Auto_shows* or *wordnet_championship*, the classifiers still can achieve very good performance, since in these cases the corresponding sets of *Flickr* photos and their associated tags are very homogeneous.

At the other end, we have the more ambiguous event classes, such as *Before_Sunrise*, *wordnet_motion*, or
wordnet_execution, for which the classification is much more difficult. For these cases (e.g. *wordnet_television_program*) even a high number of training instances does not improve much the classification accuracy. The main reason is that for these types of event classes, the underlying photo sets contain too many different types of pictures, depending on each user's understanding of the corresponding event concept. This of course, translates into a very heterogeneous tag vocabulary, which negatively influences the classification performance.

4.5 Discussion

Collaborative tagging has become an increasingly popular means for sharing and organizing resources, leading to a huge amount of user generated metadata, which can potentially provide interesting information to improve search. To tap this potential, we extended previous preliminary work with a thorough analysis of the use of tags for different collections and in different environments. We analyzed three very popular tagging systems, *Del.icio.us*, *Flickr* and *Last.fm* and investigated the type of tags users employ, their distributions inside the general tag classification scheme we proposed, as well as their suitability to improve search. Our analysis provided evidence for the usefulness of a common tag taxonomy for different collections and has shown that the distributions of tag types strongly depend on the resources they annotate. Moreover, we have shown that most of the tags can be used for search and that in most cases tagging behavior exhibits approximately the same characteristics as searching behavior. We also observed some noteworthy differences: for the music domain *Usage context/Theme* is very useful for search, yet underrepresented in the tagging material. Similarly for pictures and music *Opinion/Qualities/Mood* queries occur quite often, although people tend to neglect this category for tagging.

In general, the results indicate that for music it is easier to predict the corresponding themes of the songs rather than the moods. Comparable results for the two types of recommendations were achieved when mapping the *AllMusic.com* moods to the primary human emotions. On the other hand, mappings into the secondary human emotions are more difficult and thus are susceptible to introducing noise. Recommendations of moods for picture resources are overall of higher quality than for music, due to the much more consistent set of tags attached to the photos and used as input features. Apart from some subjective mood classes, known to be difficult to distinguish, our tag recommendations are of high quality and given the self-reinforcing nature of

4.5 Discussion

user-generated tags, suggesting opinion and usage related concepts to users results in a related tag vocabulary, which eventually will converge to a more diverse set of tags.

Another contribution of this chapter is represented by a new algorithm introduced in Section 4.4 for automatic classification of pictures into classes of events. With the method we proposed, we enable event-based indexing and browsing of photo collections, i.e. a very intuitive way of organizing one's memories. The algorithm relies entirely on collaborative created user annotations and we experiment on a subset of pictures crawled from *Flickr*. However, the approach is not restricted to this collection, but being applicable to any other photo set or other types of multimedia content (e.g. videos, music, etc.) containing similar metadata. For our experiments we rely on the YAGO event ontology, and as ground truth we made use of the *Flickr* group photo organization, taking thus the users' judgments regarding the pictures' assignment to classes of events as golden standard. We experimented with different levels of abstraction of the ontology and implicitly clustering of the original picture collection and observed that while some classes are relatively easy to learn, others require more attention or some level of disambiguation. However, which is the right level of abstraction for events, that is still understandable and accepted by users is an interesting question for further investigations. Overall, the results of our evaluations show that photo event-based classification is feasible and confirm once more the quality of the user provided tags. Moreover, these findings open new possibilities for multimedia retrieval, in particular image search.

5
Conclusions and Outlook

The amount of data available on the Web keeps growing exponentially – thus making traditional, structured organization and browsing of data impossible. Web search engines have become a commodity, such that we can not imagine the Web experience without them any more. Yet, search engines are minimally personalized for each user, if at all. At the same time, the popularity of Web 2.0 sites determined an increased participation of the large public in producing new content on its own and opened new ways for the users in sharing their experiences in form of documents (e.g., pictures, bookmarks, music, etc.). As a result, finding the right information among this vast (increasingly non-textual) amount of content available online has become a very tedious task. Moreover, there is a large discrepancy between annotations added to resources and queries used to find them, making it highly improbable to find desired results effortlessly. This chapter first summarizes our major research contributions in these areas, and then discusses some issues which remained open for future investigations.

Summary of Contributions

Textual Web IR has reached a stage where few improvements in ranking or retrieval effectiveness are foreseeable. The focus lies more on result presentation and on ranking personalization. We have shown Chapter 3 such personalization algorithms using the most valuable source of information about a user – all personal resources on the Desktop – as well as different applications.

Section 3.2 proposed Query Clarity as an indicator of user's search reformulation actions, and showed it to be more flexible than traditional approaches, which build onto naïve instruments such as the number of keywords. Moreover, we also analyzed the Part-Of-Speech transition patterns over a large search engine log.

Building upon the query reformulation analysis, in Section 3.3 we proposed to expand Web search queries by exploiting the user's Personal Information Repository in order to automatically extract additional keywords related both to the query itself and to user's interests, personalizing the search output. We proposed five techniques for determining expansion terms from personal documents. We provided a thorough empirical analysis of several variants of our approaches, under four different scenarios. We showed some of these approaches to perform very well, and our adaptive algorithm produces NDCG improvements of up to 55.62%.

We then (Section 3.4) proposed another application of the personalization algorithms: extract keywords from the user's active documents in order to describe the current user task, and present personalized recommendations. The approaches, Sentence Selection and Lexical Compounds, adapt summarization and natural language processing techniques to extract these keywords from the active document or additionally from locally stored desktop documents. We investigated their performance with respect to three types of input files, namely emails, text documents and web pages. Our experiments showed an improvement over the simple Term Frequency baseline in Mean Average Precision of 18% up to 187%.

For improving Multimedia IR we propose to use automatic semantic annotation techniques (Chapter 4) which rely on social knowledge. Collaborative tagging has become an increasingly popular means for sharing and organizing resources, leading to a huge amount of user generated metadata, which can potentially provide interesting information to improve search. In Chapter 4 we thus analyzed three very popular tagging systems, *Del.icio.us*, *Flickr* and *Last.fm* and investigated the type of tags users employ, their distributions inside the general tag classification scheme we proposed, as well as their suitability to improve search. In our analysis (Section 4.2) we observed some noteworthy differences between tagging and querying behaviors: for the music domain *Usage context/Theme* is very useful for search, yet underrepresented in the tagging material. Similarly for pictures and music *Opinion/Qualities/Mood* queries occur quite often, although people tend to neglect this category for tagging.

Building on these results, in Section 4.3, we proposed a number of algorithms which aim at bridging exactly these gaps between the tagging and querying vocabularies, by automatically recommending mood and theme annotations. We trained multi-class classifiers on input features consisting of either only the existing tags of the picture and music resources, or of tags and lyrics information, in case of music songs. The results of our evaluations showed that providing such automatic tag recommendations is feasible; we achieved $H@3$ rates of 88-89% for music themes and moods and up to 97% in the case of image moods.

With the rapid shift from analog to digital photography we have faced over the past years and with the advent of Social Media sites dedicated to photography, a huge amount of digital photos became available on the Web. However, advanced techniques for easily browsing and intuitively organizing these photo collections are still missing. Section 4.4 evaluates our newly developed algorithm for automatically classifying pictures into classes of events. With our method we enabled event-based indexing and browsing of photo collections, i.e. a very intuitive way of organizing one's memories, with classification accuracies of 80% for single events and 85% for event categories. The algorithm relies entirely on collaborative created user annotations and we experimented on a subset of pictures crawled from *Flickr*. However, the approach is not restricted to this collection, but being applicable to any other photo set or other types of multimedia content (e.g. videos, music, etc.) containing similar metadata.

Open Directions

In this thesis we presented a number of improvements in textual as well as in multimedia IR. Nevertheless, new research brings always new ideas of improvements over the existing ones.

Search Personalization can be further improved by performing investigations on the dependency between various query features and the optimal number of expansion terms. Designing a set of more complex combinations of these metrics in order to provide enhanced adaptivity to our algorithms will increase effectiveness. Also, analyzing other types of approaches to identify query expansion suggestions, such as applying Latent Semantic Analysis on the Desktop data seems promising.

When recommending related Web pages we want to investigate means to distinguish between different input file types and even file types categories (e.g. personal descriptive emails, specialized concise emails, articles, news, stories, novels, etc.) because of differences in the nature of the language used and the position of important keywords throughout these documents. When analyzing emails, we are investigating the means to extract only the topic related part of the email body, disregarding additional noise like introduction, signature or off-topic personal additions. Finally, we want to analyze other summarization and natural language processing techniques to extract keywords from documents.

Automatic Semantic Enrichment will benefit from further improving the algorithms and in particular the feature selection mechanisms by automatically identifying the tag types (e.g. *Topic, Author, Location,* etc.) and use them as input features for the classification. Other ideas worth investigating refer to identification of other types of information for multimedia resources, such as events, persons or locations, as well as other types of entities frequently queried against by users. Moreover, we would like to perform another type of evaluation, where the value of the inferred annotation can be measured directly by comparing the results obtained for a search engine with and without an enriched multimedia dataset. Last but not least, merging our approach with content-based methods trying to solve the same task is also worth examining.

Bibliography

[ACN+09] Rabeeh Abbasi, Sergey Chernov, Wolfgang Nejdl, Raluca Paiu, and Steffen Staab. Exploiting flickr tags and groups for finding landmark photos. In *Proceedings of the 31st European Conference on Information Retrieval (ECIR 2009)*, pages 654–661, 2009.

[AdA07] B. Thomas Adler and Luca de Alfaro. A content-driven reputation system for the wikipedia. In *WWW '07: Proceedings of the 16th international conference on World Wide Web*, pages 261–270, New York, NY, USA, 2007. ACM.

[AHS06] Melanie Aurnhammer, Peter Hanappe, and Luc Steels. Integrating collaborative tagging and emergent semantics for image retrieval. In *WWW Collaborative Web Tagging Workshop*, 2006.

[AN07] Morgan Ames and Mor Naaman. Why we tag: motivations for annotation in mobile and online media. In *Proceedings of the ACM SIGCHI Conference on Human Factors in Computing (CHI 2007)*, pages 971–980. ACM, 2007.

[APL98] James Allan, Ron Papka, and Victor Lavrenko. On-line new event detection and tracking. In *SIGIR '98: Proceedings of the 21st annual international ACM SIGIR conference on Research and development in information retrieval*, pages 37–45, Melbourne, Australia, 1998. ACM.

[AR02] James Allan and Hema Raghavan. Using part-of-speech patterns to reduce query ambiguity. In *SIGIR '02: Proceedings of the 25th annual international ACM SIGIR conference on Research and development in information retrieval*, pages 307–314, New York, NY, USA, 2002. ACM.

[AT99]   Peter G. Anick and Suresh Tipirneni. The paraphrase search assistant: terminological feedback for iterative information seeking. In *SIGIR '99: Proceedings of the 22nd annual international ACM SIGIR conference on Research and development in information retrieval*, pages 153–159, New York, NY, USA, 1999. ACM.

[BCFN07]   Alessandro Bozzon, Paul-Alexandru Chirita, Claudiu S. Firan, and Wolfgang Nejdl. Lexical analysis for modeling web query reformulation. In *SIGIR*, pages 739–740, 2007.

[BCSW07]   Holger Bast, Alexandru Chitea, Fabian Suchanek, and Ingmar Weber. ESTER: efficient search on text, entities, and relations. In *SIGIR '07: Proceedings of the 30th annual international ACM SIGIR conference on Research and development in information retrieval*, pages 671–678, New York, NY, USA, 2007. ACM.

[BDF+10]   Bodo Billerbeck, Gianluca Demartini, Claudiu S. Firan, Tereza Iofciu, and Ralf Krestel. Exploiting click-through data for entity retrieval. In *SIGIR*, 2010.

[BdVCS07] Peter Bailey, Arjen P. de Vries, Nick Craswell, and Ian Soboroff. Overview of the TREC 2007 Enterprise Track. In Ellen M. Voorhees and Lori P. Buckland, editors, *Proceedings of The Sixteenth Text REtrieval Conference, TREC 2007, Gaithersburg, Maryland, USA, November 5-9, 2007*, volume Special Publication 500-274. National Institute of Standards and Technology (NIST), 2007.

[BFK+09]   Kerstin Bischoff, Claudiu S. Firan, Cristina Kadar, Wolfgang Nejdl, and Raluca Paiu. Automatically identifying tag types. In *Proceedings of the 5th International Conference on Advanced Data Mining and Applications (ADMA 2009)*, volume 5678 of *Lecture Notes in Computer Science*, pages 31–42. Springer, 2009.

[BFNP08]   Kerstin Bischoff, Claudiu S. Firan, Wolfgang Nejdl, and Raluca Paiu. Can all tags be used for search? In *Proceedings of the 17th ACM conference on Information and knowledge management (CIKM '08)*, pages 193–202. ACM, 2008.

[BFNP09]   Kerstin Bischoff, Claudiu S. Firan, Wolfgang Nejdl, and Raluca Paiu. How do you feel about "dancing queen"?: deriving mood & theme annotations from user tags. In *Proceedings of the 2009 Joint International Conference on Digital Libraries (JCDL 2009)*, pages 285–294. ACM, 2009.

[BFNP10]   Kerstin Bischoff, Claudiu S. Firan, Wolfgang Nejdl, and Raluca Paiu. Bridging the gap between tagging and querying vocabularies: Analyses and applications for enhancing multimedia ir. *Journal of Web Semantics, Special Issue on Bridging the Gap Between Data Mining and Social Network Analysis*, 2010.

[BFP09a] Kerstin Bischoff, Claudiu S. Firan, and Raluca Paiu. Deriving music theme annotations from user tags. In *WWW*, pages 1193–1194, 2009.

[BFP+09b] Kerstin Bischoff, Claudiu S. Firan, Raluca Paiu, Wolfgang Nejdl, Cyril Laurier, and Mohamed Sordo. Music mood and theme classification – a hybrid approach. In *Proceedings of the 10th International Society for Music Information Retrieval Conference*, 2009.

[BH99] Jay Budzik and Kristian Hammond. Watson: Anticipating and contextualizing information needs. In *Proceedings of the Sixty-second Annual Meeting of the American Society for Information Science*, 1999.

[BHBK00] J. Budzik, K. J. Hammond, L. Birnbaum, and M. Krema. Beyond similarity. In *Working notes of the AAAI 2000 Workshop on AI for Web Search*. AAAI Press, 2000.

[BHST08] Paolo Bouquet, Harry Halpin, Heiko Stoermer, and Giovanni Tummarello, editors. *Proceedings of the 1st international workshop on Identity and Reference on the Semantic Web (IRSW2008) at the 5th European Semantic Web Conference (ESWC 2008), Tenerife, Spain, June 2nd, 2008*, CEUR Workshop Proceedings. CEUR-WS.org, 2008.

[BID+10] Bodo Billerbeck, Tereza Iofciu, Gianluca Demartini, Claudiu S. Firan, and Ralf Krestel. Ranking entities using web search query logs. In *European Conference on Research and Advanced Technology for Digital Libraries (ECDL)*, 2010.

[BNG09] Hila Becker, Mor Naaman, and Luis Gravano. Event identification in social media. In *WebDB: 12th International Workshop on the Web and Databases, WebDB*, Providence, Rhode Island, USA, 2009.

[Bro02] Andrei Broder. A Taxonomy of Web Search. *SIGIR Forum*, 36(2):3–10, 2002.

[BSB08] Paolo Bouquet, Heiko Stoermer, and Barbara Bazzanella. An Entity Name System (ENS) for the Semantic Web. In Sean Bechhofer, Manfred Hauswirth, Jörg Hoffmann, and Manolis Koubarakis, editors, *The Semantic Web: Research and Applications, 5th European Semantic Web Conference, ESWC 2008, Tenerife, Canary Islands, Spain, June 1-5, 2008, Proceedings*, volume 5021 of *Lecture Notes in Computer Science*, pages 258–272. Springer, 2008.

BIBLIOGRAPHY

[BSTH07] Paolo Bouquet, Heiko Stoermer, Giovanni Tummarello, and Harry Halpin, editors. *Proceedings of the WWW2007 Workshop I^3: Identity, Identifiers, Identification, Entity-Centric Approaches to Information and Knowledge Management on the Web, Banff, Canada, May 8, 2007*, volume 249 of *CEUR Workshop Proceedings*. CEUR-WS.org, 2007.

[Bus45] Vannevar Bush. As we may think. *The Atlantic Monthly*, July 1945.

[BWF+07] Shenghua Bao, Xiaoyuan Wu, Ben Fei, Guirong Xue, Zhong Su, and Yong Yu. Optimizing web search using social annotations. In *Proceedings of the 16th International World Wide Web Conference (WWW2007)*, 2007.

[BYRN99] Ricardo A. Baeza-Yates and Berthier A. Ribeiro-Neto. *Modern Information Retrieval*. 1999.

[CC07] Tao Cheng and Kevin Chen-Chuan Chang. Entity Search Engine: Towards Agile Best-Effort Information Integration over the Web. In *CIDR 2007, Third Biennial Conference on Innovative Data Systems Research, Asilomar, CA, USA, January 7-10, 2007, Online Proceedings*, pages 108–113. www.crdrdb.org, 2007.

[CdMRB01] Claudio Carpineto, Renato de Mori, Giovanni Romano, and Brigitte Bigi. An information-theoretic approach to automatic query expansion. *ACM Transactions on Information Systems*, 19(1):1–27, 2001.

[CFN06a] Paul Alexandru Chirita, Claudiu Firan, and Wolfgang Nejdl. Summarizing local context to personalize global web search. In *Proc. of the 15th Intl. CIKM Conf. on Information and Knowledge Management*, 2006.

[CFN06b] Paul Alexandru Chirita, Claudiu S. Firan, and Wolfgang Nejdl. Pushing task relevant web links down to the desktop. In *Proc. of the 8th ACM Intl. Workshop on Web Information and Data Management held at the 15th Intl. ACM CIKM Conf. on Information and Knowledge Management*, 2006.

[CFN07] Paul-Alexandru Chirita, Claudiu S. Firan, and Wolfgang Nejdl. Personalized query expansion for the web. In *SIGIR*, pages 7–14, 2007.

[CFPS02] David Carmel, Eitan Farchi, Yael Petruschka, and Aya Soffer. Automatic query wefinement using lexical affinities with maximal information gain. In *Proc. of the 25th Intl. ACM SIGIR Conf. on Research and development in information retrieval*, pages 283–290, 2002.

[CG98] Jaime Carbonell and Jade Goldstein. The use of mmr, diversity-based reranking for reordering documents and producing summaries. In *Proc.*

of the 21st Intl. ACM SIGIR Conf. on Research and Development in Information Retrieval, 1998.

[CH98] Chia-Hui Chang and Ching-Chi Hsu. Integrating query expansion and conceptual relevance feedback for personalized web information retrieval. In *Proc. of the 7th Intl. Conf. on World Wide Web*, 1998.

[CHN08] Ling Chen, Yiqun Hu, and Wolfgang Nejdl. Deck: Detecting events from web click-through data. In *ICDM '08: Proceedings of the 2008 Eighth IEEE International Conference on Data Mining*, pages 123–132, Washington, DC, USA, 2008. IEEE Computer Society.

[CLWB00] Mark Claypool, Phong Le, Makoto Waseda, and David Brown. Implicit interest indicators. In *Proceedings of the ACM Intelligent User Interfaces Conference (IUI)*, pages 33–40. ACM, 2000.

[Coh60] Jacob Cohen. A coefficient of agreement for nominal scales. *Educational and Psychological Measurement*, 20(1):37–46, 1960.

[CR09] Ling Chen and Abhishek Roy. Event detection from flickr data through wavelet-based spatial analysis. In *CIKM '09: Proceeding of the 18th ACM conference on Information and knowledge management*, pages 523–532, Hong Kong, China, 2009. ACM.

[CST98] I. B. Crabtree, S. Soltysiak, and M. Thint. Adaptive personal agents. *Personal Technologies*, 2(3):141–151, 1998.

[CTZC02] Steve Cronen-Townsend, Yun Zhou, and W. Bruce Croft. Predicting query performance. In *Proc. of the 25th Intl. ACM SIGIR Conf. on Research and Development in Inf. Retr.*, 2002.

[CWN09] L. Chen, P. Wright, and W. Nejdl. Improving music genre classification using collaborative tagging data. In *Proceedings of the 2nd ACM International Conference on Web Search and Data Mining (WSDM 2009)*, pages 84–93. ACM, 2009.

[CWNM02] Hang Cui, Ji-Rong Wen, Jian-Yun Nie, and Wei-Ying Ma. Probabilistic query expansion using query logs. In *Proc. of the 11th Intl. Conf. on World Wide Web*, 2002.

[CYC07] Tao Cheng, Xifeng Yan, and Kevin Chen-Chuan Chang. EntityRank: Searching Entities Directly and Holistically. In *VLDB '07: Proceedings of the 33rd international conference on Very large data bases*, pages 387–398. VLDB Endowment, 2007.

[CYTS05] David Carmel, Elad Yom-Tov, and Ian Soboroff. SIGIR workshop report: predicting query difficulty - methods and applications. *SIGIR Forum*, 39(2):25–28, 2005.

[CZG+09] David Carmel, Naama Zwerdling, Ido Guy, Shila Ofek-Koifman, Nadav Har'el, Inbal Ronen, Erel Uziel, Sivan Yogev, and Sergey Chernov. Personalized social search based on the user's social network. In *Proceedings of the 18th ACM conference on Information and knowledge management (CIKM '09)*, pages 1227–1236. ACM, 2009.

[DFG+09] Gianluca Demartini, Claudiu S. Firan, Mihai Georgescu, Tereza Iofciu, Ralf Krestel, and Wolfgang Nejdl. An architecture for finding entities on the web. In *LA-WEB/CLIHC*, pages 230–237, 2009.

[DFI07] Gianluca Demartini, Claudiu S. Firan, and Tereza Iofciu. L3s at inex 2007: Query expansion for entity ranking using a highly accurate ontology. In *INEX*, pages 252–263, 2007.

[DFI+08] Gianluca Demartini, Claudiu S. Firan, Tereza Iofciu, Ralf Krestel, and Wolfgang Nejdl. A model for ranking entities and its application to wikipedia. In *LA-WEB*, pages 29–38, 2008.

[DFI+10] Gianluca Demartini, Claudiu S. Firan, Tereza Iofciu, Ralf Krestel, , and Wolfgang Nejdl. Why finding entities in wikipedia is difficult, sometimes. *Information Retrieval Journal, Special Issue on Focused Retrieval and Results Aggregation*, 2010.

[DFIN08] Gianluca Demartini, Claudiu S. Firan, Tereza Iofciu, and Wolfgang Nejdl. Semantically enhanced entity ranking. In *WISE*, pages 176–188, 2008.

[DKM+06] Micah Dubinko, Ravi Kumar, Joseph Magnani, Jasmine Novak, Prabhakar Raghavan, and Andrew Tomkins. Visualizing tags over time. In *Proceedings of the 15th International World Wide Web Conference (WWW2006)*, pages 193–202. ACM, 2006.

[DNBL08] Peter Dunker, Stefanie Nowak, André Begau, and Cornelia Lanz. Content-based mood classification for photos and music: a generic multimodal classification framework and evaluation approach. In *Proceedings of the 1st ACM international conference on Multimedia information retrieval (MIR'08)*, pages 97–104. ACM, 2008.

[Dun93] Ted Dunning. Accurate methods for the statistics of surprise and coincidence. *Computational Linguistics*, 19:61–74, 1993.

[Edm69] H. P. Edmundson. New methods in automatic extracting. *Journal of the ACM*, 16(2):264–285, 1969.

[Eft95]	Efthimis N. Efthimiadis. User choices: A new yardstick for the evaluation of ranking algorithms for interactive query expansion. *Information Processing and Management*, 31(4):605–620, 1995.
[ELBMG07]	D. Eck, P. Lamere, T. Bertin-Mahieux, and S. Green. Automatic generation of social tags for music recommendation. In *Advances in Neural Information Processing Systems 20, Proceedings of the Twenty-First Annual Conference on Neural Information Processing Systems (NIPS)*. MIT Press, 2007.
[Elo95]	S. Elo. Plum: Contextualizing news for communities through augmentation, 1995.
[EO79]	P. Ekman and H. Oster. Facial expressions of emotion. *Annu. Rev. Psychol.*, 30:527–554, 1979.
[ER04]	Günes Erkan and Dragomir R. Radev. Lexrank: Graph-based lexical centrality as salience in text summarization. *J. Artif. Intell. Res. (JAIR)*, 22:457–479, 2004.
[FGNP10]	Claudiu S. Firan, Mihai Georgescu, Wolfgang Nejdl, and Raluca Paiu. Bringing order to your photos: Event-driven classification of flickr images based on social knowledge. In *Proceedings of the 19th International Conference on Information and Knowledge Management*, 2010.
[FL03]	B. Fasel and J. Luettin. Automatic facial expression analysis: a survey. *Pattern Recognition*, 36(1):259–275, 2003.
[FNP07]	Claudiu S. Firan, Wolfgang Nejdl, and Raluca Paiu. The benefit of using tag-based profiles. In *LA-WEB*, pages 32–41, 2007.
[FR05]	Daniel Fogaras and Balazs Racz. Scaling link based similarity search. In *Proc. of the 14th Intl. World Wide Web Conf.*, 2005.
[FYYL05]	Gabriel Pui Cheong Fung, Jeffrey Xu Yu, Philip S. Yu, and Hongjun Lu. Parameter free bursty events detection in text streams. In *VLDB '05: Proceedings of the 31st international conference on Very large data bases*, pages 181–192, Trondheim, Norway, 2005. VLDB Endowment.
[FZP03]	Yazhong Feng, Yueting Zhuang, and Yunhe Pan. Popular music retrieval by detecting mood. In *Proceedings of the 26th Annual International ACM SIGIR Conference on Research and Development in Information Retrieval (SIGIR 2003)*. ACM, 2003.
[GCC+08]	Julien Gaugaz, Stefania Costache, Paul-Alexandru Chirita, Claudiu S. Firan, and Wolfgang Nejdl. Activity based links as a ranking factor in semantic desktop search. In *LA-WEB*, pages 49–57, 2008.

[GH06]   Scott A. Golder and Bernardo A. Huberman. Usage patterns of collaborative tagging systems. *Journal of Information Science*, 32(2):198–208, 2006.

[GKMC99]   Jade Goldstein, Mark Kantrowitz, Vibhu Mittal, and Jaime Carbonell. Summarizing text documents: Sentence selection and evaluation metrics. In *Proc. of the 22nd Intl. ACM SIGIR Conf. on Research and Development in Information Retrieval*, 1999.

[Hav02]   T. Haveliwala. Topic-sensitive pagerank. In *Proc. of the 11th Intl. World Wide Web Conf., Honolulu, Hawaii*, May 2002.

[HCL07]   Qi He, Kuiyu Chang, and Ee-Peng Lim. Analyzing feature trajectories for event detection. In *SIGIR '07: Proceedings of the 30th annual international ACM SIGIR conference on Research and development in information retrieval*, pages 207–214, Amsterdam, The Netherlands, 2007. ACM.

[HJSS06]   Andreas Hotho, Robert Jäschke, Christoph Schmitz, and Gerd Stumme. Information retrieval in folksonomies: Search and ranking. In *The Semantic Web: Research and Applications, Proceedings of the 3rd European Semantic Web Conference (ESWC 2006)*, volume 4011 of *Lecture Notes in Computer Science*, pages 411–426. Springer, 2006.

[HKGM08]   Paul Heymann, Georgia Koutrika, and Hector Garcia-Molina. Can social bookmarking improve web search? In *Proceedings of the 1st ACM International Conference on Web Search and Data Mining (WSDM 2008)*. ACM, 2008.

[HM08]   Tom Heath and Enrico Motta. Revyu: Linking reviews and ratings into the Web of Data. *J. Web Sem.*, 6(4):266–273, 2008.

[HO04]   B. He and I. Ounis. Inferring query performance using pre-retrieval predictors. In *Proc. of the 11th Intl. SPIRE Conf. on String Processing and Information Retrieval*, 2004.

[HRGM08]   Paul Heymann, Daniel Ramage, and Hector Garcia-Molina. Social tag prediction. In *Proceedings of the 31th Annual International ACM SIGIR Conference on Research and Development in Information Retrieval (SIGIR 2008)*, 2008.

[HRS07]   Harry Halpin, Valentin Robu, and Hana Shepherd. The complex dynamics of collaborative tagging. In *Proceedings of the 16th International World Wide Web Conference (WWW2007)*, pages 211–220. ACM, 2007.

[JF03]	Rosie Jones and Daniel C. Fain. Query word deletion prediction. In *Proc. of the 26th Intl. ACM SIGIR Conf. on Research and Development in Informaion Retrieval*, 2003.
[JFM97]	T. Joachims, D. Freitag, and T. Mitchell. Webwatcher: A tour guide for the world wide web. In *Proceedings of IJCAI97*, 1997.
[JK00]	K. Järvelin and J. Keklinen. Ir evaluation methods for retrieving highly relevant documents. In *Proc. of the 23th Intl. ACM SIGIR Conf. on Research and development in information retrieval*, 2000.
[JW03]	G. Jeh and J. Widom. Scaling personalized web search. In *Proc. of the 12th Intl. World Wide Web Conference*, 2003.
[JWR98]	K. Sparck Jones, S. Walker, and S. Robertson. Probabilistic model of information retrieval: Development and status. Technical report, Cambridge University, 1998.
[Kat96]	S. Katz. Distribution of content words and phrases in text and language modelling. *Natural Language Engineering*, 2(1):15–59, 1996.
[KC92]	Robert Krovetz and W. Bruce Croft. Lexical ambiguity and information retrieval. *ACM Trans. Inf. Syst.*, 10(2), 1992.
[KC99]	Myoung-Cheol Kim and Key-Sun Choi. A comparison of collocation-based similarity measures in query expansion. *Information Processing and Management*, 35(1):19–30, 1999.
[KEG+07]	Georgia Koutrika, Frans Adjie Effendi, Zoltán Gyöngyi, Paul Heymann, and Hector Garcia-Molina. Combating spam in tagging systems. In *AIRWeb '07: Proceedings of the 3rd international workshop on Adversarial information retrieval on the web*, pages 57–64, Banff, Alberta, Canada, 2007. ACM.
[KPSW07]	Peter Knees, Tim Pohle, Markus Schedl, and Gerhard Widmer. A music search engine built upon audio-based and web-based similarity measures. In *Proceedings of the 30th Annual International ACM SIGIR Conference on Research and Development in Information Retrieval (SIGIR 2007)*, pages 447–454. ACM, 2007.
[KSR04]	Sang-Bum Kim, Hee-Cheol Seo, and Hae-Chang Rim. Information retrieval using word senses: root sense tagging approach. In *Proc. of the 27th Intl. ACM SIGIR Conf. on Research and development in information retrieval*, 2004.
[KZ04]	Reiner Kraft and Jason Zien. Mining anchor text for query refinement. In *Proc. of the 13th Intl. Conf. on World Wide Web*, 2004.

[LAJ01]   Adenike M. Lam-Adesina and Gareth J. F. Jones. Applying summarization techniques for term selection in relevance feedback. In *Proc. of the 24th Intl. ACM SIGIR Conf. on Research and Development in Information Retrieval*, 2001.

[LC03]   D. Lawrie and W. Croft. Generating hierarchical summaries for web searches. In *Proc. of the 26th Intl. ACM SIGIR Conf. on Research and Development in Information Retr.*, 2003.

[LCR01]   Dawn Lawrie, W. Bruce Croft, and Arnold L. Rosenberg. Finding topic words for hierarchical summarization. In *Proc. of the 24th Intl. ACM SIGIR Conf. on Research and Development in Information Retrieval*, 2001.

[LH99]   Tessa Lau and Eric Horvitz. Patterns of search: Analyzing and modeling web query refinement. In *Proc. of the 7th Intl. Conf. on User Modeling*, 1999.

[Lie95]   H. Lieberman. Letizia: An agent that assists web browsing. In *In Proceedings of IJCAI 95*. AAAI Press, 1995.

[LK77]   J. R. Landis and G. G. Koch. The measurement of observer agreement for categorical data. *Biometrics*, 33(1):159–174, 1977.

[LLYM04] Shuang Liu, Fang Liu, Clement Yu, and Weiyi Meng. An effective approach to document retrieval via utilizing wordnet and recognizing phrases. In *Proc. of the 27th Intl. ACM SIGIR Conf. on Research and development in information retrieval*, 2004.

[LLZ03]   Dan Liu, Lie Lu, and Hong-Jiang Zhang. Automatic mood detection from acoustic music data. In *ISMIR '03: Proceedings of the 4th International Conference on Music Information Retrieval*, Washington, D.C., USA, 2003.

[LS07]   M. Levy and M. Sandler. A semantic space for music derived from social tags. In *Proceedings of the 8th International Society for Music Information Retrieval Conference (ISMIR 2007)*, 2007.

[Luh58]   H. Luhn. Automatic creation of literature abstracts. *IBM Journ. of Research and Development*, 2(2):159–165, 1958.

[LWLM05] Zhiwei Li, Bin Wang, Mingjing Li, and Wei-Ying Ma. A probabilistic model for retrospective news event detection. In *SIGIR '05: Proceedings of the 28th annual international ACM SIGIR conference on Research and development in information retrieval*, pages 106–113, Salvador, Brazil, 2005. ACM.

[MBCS00] Paul P. Maglio, Rob Barrett, Christopher S. Campbell, and Ted Selker. Suitor: an attentive information system. In *IUI '00: Proceedings of the 5th international conference on Intelligent user interfaces*, pages 169–176, New York, NY, USA, 2000. ACM Press.

[Mil95] G.A. Miller. Wordnet: An electronic lexical database. *Communications of the ACM*, 38(11):39–41, 1995.

[MNBD06] Cameron Marlow, Mor Naaman, Danah Boyd, and Marc Davis. Ht06, tagging paper, taxonomy, flickr, academic article, to read. In *Proceedings of the 17th ACM Conference on Hypertext and Hypermedia (HYPERTEXT 2006)*, pages 31–40. ACM, 2006.

[MRS08] Christopher D. Manning, Prabhakar Raghavan, and Hinrich Schütze. *Introduction to Information Retrieval*. Cambridge University Press, 2008.

[NDQ06] L. Nie, B. Davison, and X. Qi. Topical link analysis for web search. In *Proc. of the 29th Intl. ACM SIGIR Conf. on Res. and Development in Inf. Retr.*, 2006.

[NM01] Tadashi Nomoto and Yuji Matsumoto. A new approach to unsupervised text summarization. In *Proc. of the 24th Intl. ACM SIGIR Conf. on Research and Development in Information Retrieval*, 2001.

[NN08] Mor Naaman and Rahul Nair. Zonetag's collaborative tag suggestions: What is this person doing in my phone? *IEEE MultiMedia*, 15(3):34–40, 2008.

[PBMW98] Lawrence Page, Sergey Brin, Rajeev Motwani, and Terry Winograd. The pagerank citation ranking: Bringing order to the web. Technical report, Stanford University, 1998.

[PCAV08] Themis Palpanas, Junaid Chaudhry, Periklis Andritsos, and Yannis Velegrakis. Entity Data Management in OKKAM. In *DEXA '08: Proceedings of the 2008 19th International Conference on Database and Expert Systems Application*, pages 729–733, Washington, DC, USA, 2008. IEEE Computer Society.

[PCT06] Greg Pass, Abdur Chowdhury, and Cayley Torgeson. A picture of search. In *Proceedings of the 1st International Conference on Scalable Information Systems (Infoscale 2006)*. ACM, 2006.

[PFN08] Raluca Paiu, Ling Chen 0002, Claudiu S. Firan, and Wolfgang Nejdl. Pharos - personalizing users' experience in audio-visual online spaces. In *PersDB*, pages 40–47, 2008.

[PVT08] Jovan Pehcevski, Anne-Marie Vercoustre, and James A. Thom. Exploiting Locality of Wikipedia Links in Entity Ranking. In Craig Macdonald, Iadh Ounis, Vassilis Plachouras, Ian Ruthven, and Ryen W. White, editors, *Advances in Information Retrieval , 30th European Conference on IR Research, ECIR 2008, Glasgow, UK, March 30-April 3, 2008. Proceedings*, volume 4956 of *Lecture Notes in Computer Science*, pages 258–269. Springer, 2008.

[QC06] F. Qiu and J. Cho. Automatic indentification of user interest for personalized search. In *Proc. of the 15th Intl. WWW Conf.*, 2006.

[QF93] Yonggang Qiu and Hans-Peter Frei. Concept based query expansion. In *Proc. of the 16th Intl. ACM SIGIR Conf. on Research and Development in Inf. Retr.*, 1993.

[RGN07] Tye Rattenbury, Nathaniel Good, and Mor Naaman. Towards automatic extraction of event and place semantics from flickr tags. In *Proceedings of the 30th Annual International ACM SIGIR Conference on Research and Development in Information Retrieval (SIGIR 2007)*. ACM, 2007.

[Rho97] Bradley J. Rhodes. The wearable remembrance agent: A system for augmented memory. *Personal Technologies*, pages 218–224, 1997.

[Rho00] Bradley J. Rhodes. Margin notes: building a contextually aware associative memory. In *IUI '00: Proceedings of the 5th international conference on Intelligent user interfaces*, pages 219–224, New York, NY, USA, 2000. ACM Press.

[RM00] B. J. Rhodes and P. Maes. Just-in-time information retrieval agents. *IBM Syst. J.*, 39(3-4):685–704, 2000.

[Roc71] J. Rocchio. Relevance feedback in information retrieval. *The Smart Retrieval System: Experiments in Automatic Document Processing*, pages 313–323, 1971.

[RS96] Bradley Rhodes and Thad Starner. The remembrance agent: A continuously running automated information retrieval system. In *The Proceedings of The First International Conference on The Practical Application of Intelligent Agents and Multi Agent Technology (PAAM '96)*, pages 487–495, 1996.

[RSS08] Yves Raimond, Christopher Sutton, and Mark Sandler. Automatic Interlinking of Music Datasets on the Semantic Web. In *Linked Data on the Web (LDOW2008)*, 2008.

[RTK06]   Thomas Rölleke, Theodora Tsikrika, and Gabriella Kazai. A general matrix framework for modelling information retrieval. *Inf. Process. Manage.*, 42(1):4–30, 2006.

[Rut03]   Ian Ruthven. Re-examining the potential effectiveness of interactive query expansion. In *Proc. of the 26th Intl. ACM SIGIR Conf. on Research and development in informaion retrieval*, 2003.

[Sal88]   Gerald Salton, editor. *Automatic text processing*. Addison-Wesley Longman Publishing Co., Inc., Boston, MA, USA, 1988.

[SBC+06]   Tamas Sarlos, Andras A. Benczur, Karoly Csalogany, Daniel Fogaras, and Balazs Racz. To randomize or not to randomize: Space optimal summaries for hyperlink analysis. In *Proc. of the 15th Intl. WWW Conf.*, 2006.

[SC99]   Mark Sanderson and W. Bruce Croft. Deriving concept hierarchies from text. In *Proc. of the 22nd Intl. ACM SIGIR Conf. on Research and Development in Information Retr.*, 1999.

[SC04]   Chirag Shah and W. Bruce Croft. Evaluating high accuracy retrieval techniques. In *Proc. of the 27th Intl. ACM SIGIR Conf. on Research and development in information retrieval*, pages 2–9, 2004.

[SHY04]   Kazunari Sugiyama, Kenji Hatano, and Masatoshi Yoshikawa. Adaptive web search based on user profile constructed without any effort from users. In *Proc. of the 13th Intl. WWW Conf.*, 2004.

[SKW07]   Fabian M. Suchanek, Gjergji Kasneci, and Gerhard Weikum. Yago: a core of semantic knowledge. In Carey L. Williamson, Mary Ellen Zurko, Peter F. Patel-Schneider, and Prashant J. Shenoy, editors, *Proceedings of the 16th International Conference on World Wide Web, WWW 2007, Banff, Alberta, Canada, May 8-12, 2007*, pages 697–706. ACM, 2007.

[SLR+06]   Shilad Sen, Shyong K. Lam, Al Mamunur Rashid, Dan Cosley, Dan Frankowski, Jeremy Osterhouse, F. Maxwell Harper, and John Riedl. tagging, communities, vocabulary, evolution. In *Proceedings of the 2006 ACM Conference on Computer Supported Cooperative Work (CSCW 2006)*, pages 181–190. ACM, 2006.

[SOHB07]   Sanjay Sood, Sara Owsley, Kristian Hammond, and Larry Birnbaum. Tagassist: Automatic tag suggestion for blog posts. In *Proceedings of the International Conference on Weblogs and Social Media (ICWSM 2007)*, 2007.

[SSKO87]   Phillip Shaver, Judith Schwartz, Donald Kirson, and Cary O'Connor. Emotion knowledge: Further exploration of a prototype approach. *Journal of Personality and Social Psychology*, 52(6):1061–1086, 1987.

[Sul04]   Danny Sullivan. The older you are, the more you want personalized search, 2004. http://searchenginewatch.com/searchday/article.php/3385131.

[SvZ08]   Brkur Sigurbjörnsson and Roelof van Zwol. Flickr tag recommendation based on collective knowledge. In *Proceedings of the 17th World Wide Web Conference (WWW2008)*. ACM, 2008.

[SWJS01]   Amanda Spink, Dietmar Wolfram, Major B. J. Jansen, and Tefko Saracevic. Searching the web: the public and their queries. *J. Amer. Soc. Inf. Sci. Technol.*, 52(3):226–234, 2001.

[TDH05]   Jaime Teevan, Susan Dumais, and Eric Horvitz. Personalizing search via automated analysis of interests and activities. In *Proc. of the 28th Intl. ACM SIGIR Conf. on Research and Development in Information Retrieval*, 2005.

[tdt]   Topic detection and tracking evaluation. http://www.itl.nist.gov/iad/mig//tests/tdt/.

[Tha89]   R. E. Thayer. *The biopsychology of mood and arousal.* Oxford University Press, 1989.

[TSR+08]   Theodora Tsikrika, Pavel Serdyukov, Henning Rode, Thijs Westerveld, Robin Aly, Djoerd Hiemstra, and Arjen P. Vries. Structured Document Retrieval, Multimedia Retrieval, and Entity Ranking Using PF/Tijah. In *Focused Access to XML Documents: 6th International Workshop of the Initiative for the Evaluation of XML Retrieval, INEX 2007 Dagstuhl Castle, Germany, December 17-19, 2007. Selected Papers*, pages 306–320, Berlin, Heidelberg, 2008. Springer-Verlag.

[Vol00]   Eugene Volokh. Personalization and privacy. *Commun. ACM*, 43(8), 2000.

[Voo94]   Ellen M. Voorhees. Query expansion using lexical-semantic relations. In *Proc. of the 17th Intl. ACM SIGIR Conf. on Res. and development in Inf. Retr.*, 1994.

[VPN09]   Anne-Marie Vercoustre, Jovan Pehcevski, and Vladimir Naumovski. Topic Difficulty Prediction in Entity Ranking. In *Advances in Focused*

Retrieval: 7th International Workshop of the Initiative for the Evaluation of XML Retrieval, INEX 2008, Dagstuhl Castle, Germany, December 15-18, 2008. Revised and Selected Papers, pages 280–291, Berlin, Heidelberg, 2009. Springer-Verlag.

[WRB+98] S. Walker, S. Robertson, M. Boughanem, G. Jones, and K. Sparck Jones. Okapi at trec-6. *NIST Special Publication*, 1998.

[XC96] Jinxi Xu and W. Bruce Croft. Query expansion using local and global document analysis. In *Proc. of the 19th Intl. ACM SIGIR Conf. on Research and Development in Information Retrieval*, 1996.

[XFMS06] Zhichen Xu, Yun Fu, Jianchang Mao, and Difu Su. Towards the semantic web: Collaborative tag suggestions. In *Workshop on Collaborative Web Tagging, held at the 15th International World Wide Web Conference*, 2006.

[YCWM03] Shipeng Yu, Deng Cai, Ji-Rong Wen, and Wei-Ying Ma. Improving pseudo-relevance feedback in web information retrieval using web page segmentation. In *Proc. of the 12th Intl. Conf. on World Wide Web*, 2003.

[YPC98] Yiming Yang, Tom Pierce, and Jaime Carbonell. A study of retrospective and on-line event detection. In *SIGIR '98: Proceedings of the 21st annual international ACM SIGIR conference on Research and development in information retrieval*, pages 28–36, Melbourne, Australia, 1998. ACM.

[ZHC+04] Hua-Jun Zeng, Qi-Cai He, Zheng Chen, Wei-Ying Ma, and Jinwen Ma. Learning to cluster web search results. In *Proc. of the 27th Intl. ACM SIGIR Conf. on Research and Development in Information Retrieval*, 2004.

[ZNS08] Cäcilia Zirn, Vivi Nastase, and Michael Strube. Distinguishing between Instances and Classes in the Wikipedia Taxonomy. In Sean Bechhofer, Manfred Hauswirth, Jörg Hoffmann, and Manolis Koubarakis, editors, *The Semantic Web: Research and Applications, 5th European Semantic Web Conference, ESWC 2008, Tenerife, Canary Islands, Spain, June 1-5, 2008, Proceedings*, volume 5021 of *Lecture Notes in Computer Science*, pages 376–387. Springer, 2008.

[Zol07] Alla Zollers. Emerging motivations for tagging: Expression, performance, and activism. In *Workshop on Tagging and Metadata for Social Information Organization, held at the 16th International World Wide Web Conference*, 2007.

[ZRM+07] Hugo Zaragoza, Henning Rode, Peter Mika, Jordi Atserias, Massimiliano Ciaramita, and Giuseppe Attardi. Ranking very many typed Entities on Wikipedia. In *CIKM '07: Proceedings of the sixteenth ACM conference on Conference on information and knowledge management*, pages 1015–1018, New York, NY, USA, 2007. ACM.

Die VDM Verlagsservicegesellschaft sucht für wissenschaftliche Verlage abgeschlossene und herausragende

Dissertationen, Habilitationen, Diplomarbeiten, Master Theses, Magisterarbeiten usw.

für die kostenlose Publikation als Fachbuch.

Sie verfügen über eine Arbeit, die hohen inhaltlichen und formalen Ansprüchen genügt, und haben Interesse an einer honorarvergüteten Publikation?

Dann senden Sie bitte erste Informationen über sich und Ihre Arbeit per Email an *info@vdm-vsg.de*.

Sie erhalten kurzfristig unser Feedback!

VDM Verlagsservicegesellschaft mbH
Dudweiler Landstr. 99   Telefon +49 681 3720 174
D - 66123 Saarbrücken   Fax   +49 681 3720 1749
www.vdm-vsg.de

Die VDM Verlagsservicegesellschaft mbH vertritt

Printed by Books on Demand GmbH, Norderstedt / Germany